Eyewitness
POND & RIVER

Swan mussel shell

Common reed

Common reed
fruiting head

Water snail shell

Otter skull

Mayfly

Kingfisher skull

Reedmace
fruit

Reed bunting nest
and eggs

Mallard egg

Great diving beetle

Kingfisher wing

Bittern egg

Snipe egg

Banded demoiselle
damselfly

Great ramshorn shell

Eyewitness
POND & RIVER

In association with
THE NATURAL HISTORY MUSEUM

Written by
STEVE PARKER

Wandering
snail shells

Trout

Great pond snail shell

Hornwort

Tufted duck skull

Southern hawker
dragonfly

Teasel heads

Pintail feather

Curly waterweed

Floating pondweed leaves

River snail

Fern

Yellow flag seeds

Waterbird feather

Water beetle

Bog pondweed leaves

DK

LONDON, NEW YORK, MELBOURNE, MUNICH, and DELHI

Project editor Sophie Mitchell
Art editor Pamela Harrington
Managing art editor Jane Owen
Special photography Philip Dowell
Picture researcher Millie Trowbridge
Editorial consultants
The staff of the Natural History Museum, London

THIS EDITION
Editors Karen O'Brien, Steve Setford, Jessamy Wood
Art editors Ann Cannings, Peter Radcliffe
Senior editor Kitty Blount
Senior art editor Martin Wilson
Managing editors Julie Ferris, Jane Yorke
Managing art editors Owen Peyton Jones, Jane Thomas
Associate publisher Andrew Macintyre
Production editors Andy Hilliard, Jenny Jacoby, Hitesh Patel
Picture researchers Lorna Ainger, Harriet Mills
DTP designer Siu Yin Ho
Jacket editor Adam Powley

This Eyewitness ® Guide has been conceived by
Dorling Kindersley Limited and Editions Gallimard

First published in Great Britain in 1988
This revised edition published in Great Britain in 2011 by
Dorling Kindersley Limited,
80 Strand, London WC2R ORL

Copyright © 1988, 2003, 2011 Dorling Kindersley Limited, London
A Penguin Company

2 4 6 8 10 9 7 5 3 1

175400 – 01/11

A CIP catalogue record for this book is
available from the British Library.

ISBN 978-1-40534-539-2

Colour reproduction by Colourscan,
Singapore; MDP, UK

Printed and bound by Toppan Printing Co.
(Shenzhen) Ltd, China

Azolla water fern

Water boatman

Dragonfly larva

Water starwort

Three-spined sticklebacks

Waterbird feather

Water-lily leaves

Marestail

Discover more at
www.dk.com

Great pond snails

Hornwort

Contents

Great ramshorn shell

Fool's watercress leaf

Hornwort leaf

Spring plants

Aﬀter the dull, cold days of winter, spring is here at last. The days are lengthening and temperatures are rising. For plants, it is the beginning of the annual race to occupy a sunny position. In general, the tiny algae, duckweeds, and other small plants are the first to show their growth, since each individual plant is small and needs relatively few nutrients to increase in size. But around the pond, and in marshy areas elsewhere, the irises, reeds, and other colonizers are also showing new green shoots and leaves. All the plants shown below were collected from around a pond on a spring day – they give an idea of the species you may find, although there will always be variations from pond to pond.

☞ **WARNING**
All the plants and animals shown in this book were collected only after gaining permission from the relevant organizations. Always observe the wildlife and country codes when collecting specimens. ☜

Water crowfoot, one of the first pond flowers to appear in spring

Mature male flowerhead

Great pond sedge

REEDS REBORN
New shoots of reed grass spring up from a tangle of rooting stems and roots, in the marshy area adjacent to the pond or river. One of last year's stems still stands erect, as tall as a person.

Immature female flowerhead

Last year's stem persists through the winter

Common sedge

Reed grass

POLLEN AT ITS TIP
This great pond sedge already has one of the male flowerheads at its tip, with stamens open and shedding yellow pollen. The female flowerheads are carried lower on the stem; these are not yet mature.

SEDGE AT THE EDGE
Beside the pond grows common sedge, its flowerheads not yet fully open.

SPRING LILAC
Some of the earliest splashes of colour around the pond are the pale lilac blooms of the cuckoo flower, or lady's smock.

Cuckoo flower

New spring growth

SEASON OF CATKINS
Willows, common trees of lake and river edges, greet spring with a fine display of furry catkins. These are the tree's flowers. Early bees and other insects visit the flowers for nectar and pollen, and act as pollinators. The wind also blows pollen from the golden male catkins to the greenish female ones, which are usually borne on a different tree.

Female catkin

Goat (pussy) willow

Weeping willow

Female catkin

Crack willow

FLAGS STILL FURLED
This yellow flag iris will soon be in bloom. Here, the new leaves grow up from the thick, spreading, underground stem. Their sword-like shape has given this plant the alternative name of sword flag.

Yellow flag

Sword-like leaf

PUSS MOTH
The caterpillar of the puss moth feeds on sallow (a kind of willow) and poplar leaves. Both these trees are common in damp or moist soils, so puss moths and their caterpillars are often seen near ponds and rivers.

Male catkin covered in yellow pollen

Last year's stem

KING OF THE FLOWERS
The brilliant yellow flowers of the marsh marigold, or kingcup, decorate pond edges and other damp areas almost as soon as the snows melt away. A herbivore, such as a snail, has already made a meal of one new leaf.

WATER PLANTAIN
A pale, woody stem is all that is left of last year's 1-m (3-ft) high spray of flowers (p.57). New leaves grow from a bulb-like base. Despite its name, the water plantain is not one of the true plantains, which are the bane of the keen lawn gardener.

New spring growth

Marsh marigold

Leaf damaged by snail

Meadow rue

Delicate, notched leaves

Water plantain

SPRING FLUSH
A young meadow rue bears its first flush of distinctively notched leaves. It prefers damp meadows and pond or stream banks.

Spring animals

As THE SPRING SUN'S WARMTH spreads through the water, animals begin to stir themselves from among the weeds and mud at the bottom of the pond. It is a time of urgent new life. Frogs, toads, fish, and newts, are courting, mating, and laying eggs. Their offspring soon hatch in the warming water, eager to cash in on the spring burst of life that provides food for all. Cold-blooded aquatic creatures become more active with the rising water temperature, and in a mild spring the smaller ponds, which warm up faster than large ones, are soon seething with newly hatched snails, insects, amphibians, and many other creatures.

Frogspawn

Protective jelly surrounding egg

Black egg

Engraving of a water flea, showing its complex anatomy

Tiny tadpole from a cool pond

Tadpole from a warm pond

THE SPAWN IS BORN
As early as January, adult frogs gather in ponds and prepare to spawn (pp.38–39). Around March, the female lays up to 3,000 eggs, fertilized by the male, who clings to her back. The water-absorbing jelly around each egg swells, and soon the whole mass is many times her body size.

BIG BROTHERS AND SISTERS
Tadpoles hatch from spawn some two to three weeks after being laid. The warmer the water, the faster they develop. Here, common frog tadpoles from a large, cool pond, only two weeks out of their eggs, mingle with four-weekers from a small pond that warmed up more quickly.

One-year-old common toad

Dry, warty skin

BORN ON TO THEIR FOOD
Each adult pond snail lays up to 400 eggs, embedded in a rope-like jelly attached to the underside of a submerged leaf, on which the young snails will feed (p.52).

A NEW LEAF
In spring, water snails lay their eggs under leaves, like these water-lily leaves.

Water-lily leaves

Protective jelly

Snail egg

Pond snail

Water flea

SPRING BLOOM
Water fleas and other minute animals and plants bring a pea-green-soup look to many ponds in spring. This is the early growth of micro-organisms that provides food for larger creatures.

TWO SEXES IN ONE
Many adult pond snails are hermaphrodites, which means they have both male and female reproductive organs.

Damage to leaf edge caused by natural splitting

SECOND SPRING
This young water beetle, common in small ponds and ditches, may well be celebrating its second birthday. Two years ago it was an egg, in that autumn a larva, last spring a pupa, and last summer a newly emerged adult.

FIRST SPRING
A water beetle larva has large jaws that it can thrust forwards to snatch any edible small creatures that the spring pond has to offer. Some species stay as larvae for two years or more before pupating into adults (p.51).

KING OF THE BEETLES
The great diving beetle is the king of the carnivores in many small ponds, feeding on tadpoles, small fish, and almost anything else it can catch. In fact, the dull, furrowed wing covers on the back of this beetle indicate that it is not a king, but a queen – a female. The male's wing cases are smooth and shiny.

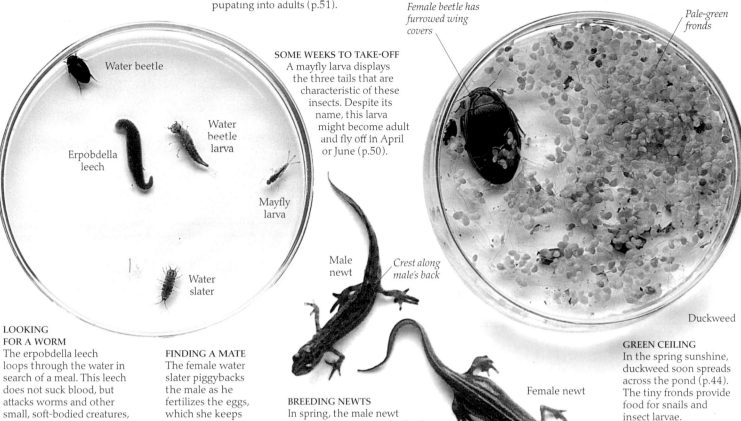

Female beetle has furrowed wing covers

Pale-green fronds

Water beetle

SOME WEEKS TO TAKE-OFF
A mayfly larva displays the three tails that are characteristic of these insects. Despite its name, this larva might become adult and fly off in April or June (p.50).

Water beetle larva

Erpobdella leech

Mayfly larva

Male newt

Crest along male's back

Water slater

Duckweed

LOOKING FOR A WORM
The erpobdella leech loops through the water in search of a meal. This leech does not suck blood, but attacks worms and other small, soft-bodied creatures, which it swallows whole.

FINDING A MATE
The female water slater piggybacks the male as he fertilizes the eggs, which she keeps in a pouch under her body.

BREEDING NEWTS
In spring, the male newt develops a crest along his back and black spots over his skin. The female's skin remains olive-brown.

Female newt

GREEN CEILING
In the spring sunshine, duckweed soon spreads across the pond (p.44). The tiny fronds provide food for snails and insect larvae.

One-year-old common frog

Smooth, shiny skin

EARLY FLOWERS
The water crowfoot is an aquatic type of buttercup. The broad, flat leaves that float on the surface shade the water beneath, providing a good hiding place for fish.

ONE-YEAR-OLDS
Apart from breeding adults, spawn, and tadpoles, you may also find last year's babies around the pond in spring (pp.38–39).

Broad, flat leaf floats on the surface

READY TO MATE
In spring, the male stickleback's throat and underside turn bright red (a red tinge can even be seen from above, as on the male shown here). In this breeding colouration, he entices the female to lay eggs in the nest he has built on the pond bed (p.25).

Young frog that has lost its tail

Finely divided underwater leaf

Male stickleback

Female stickleback

Early summer plants

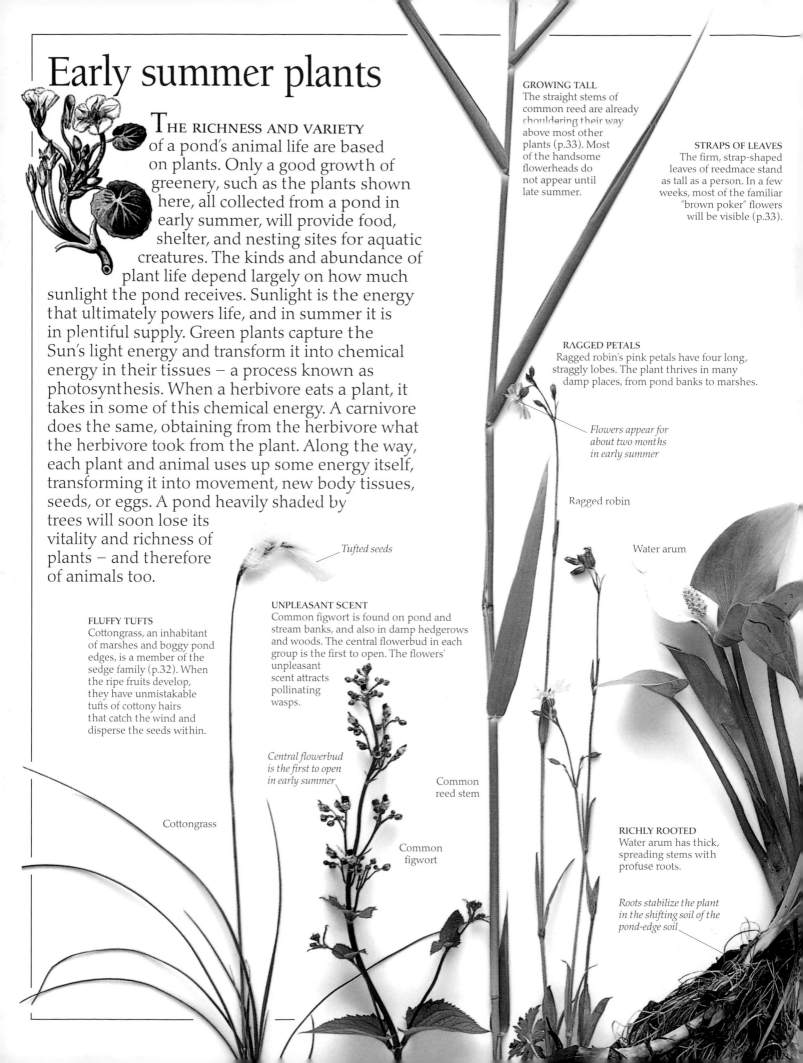

THE RICHNESS AND VARIETY of a pond's animal life are based on plants. Only a good growth of greenery, such as the plants shown here, all collected from a pond in early summer, will provide food, shelter, and nesting sites for aquatic creatures. The kinds and abundance of plant life depend largely on how much sunlight the pond receives. Sunlight is the energy that ultimately powers life, and in summer it is in plentiful supply. Green plants capture the Sun's light energy and transform it into chemical energy in their tissues – a process known as photosynthesis. When a herbivore eats a plant, it takes in some of this chemical energy. A carnivore does the same, obtaining from the herbivore what the herbivore took from the plant. Along the way, each plant and animal uses up some energy itself, transforming it into movement, new body tissues, seeds, or eggs. A pond heavily shaded by trees will soon lose its vitality and richness of plants – and therefore of animals too.

GROWING TALL
The straight stems of common reed are already shouldering their way above most other plants (p.33). Most of the handsome flowerheads do not appear until late summer.

STRAPS OF LEAVES
The firm, strap-shaped leaves of reedmace stand as tall as a person. In a few weeks, most of the familiar "brown poker" flowers will be visible (p.33).

RAGGED PETALS
Ragged robin's pink petals have four long, straggly lobes. The plant thrives in many damp places, from pond banks to marshes.

Flowers appear for about two months in early summer

Ragged robin

Water arum

Tufted seeds

FLUFFY TUFTS
Cottongrass, an inhabitant of marshes and boggy pond edges, is a member of the sedge family (p.32). When the ripe fruits develop, they have unmistakable tufts of cottony hairs that catch the wind and disperse the seeds within.

UNPLEASANT SCENT
Common figwort is found on pond and stream banks, and also in damp hedgerows and woods. The central flowerbud in each group is the first to open. The flowers' unpleasant scent attracts pollinating wasps.

Central flowerbud is the first to open in early summer

Cottongrass

Common figwort

Common reed stem

RICHLY ROOTED
Water arum has thick, spreading stems with profuse roots.

Roots stabilize the plant in the shifting soil of the pond-edge soil

RIPENING FRUITS
The grey willow's leaves are more rounded than the spear-shaped leaves of weeping willow. This tree, also called the sallow, is developing fluff-covered fruits from the female catkins (p.7). Like most willows, it roots well in damp ground by ponds and rivers.

EMERGING FLOWERS
The yellow flag iris has yellow flowers that are just beginning to unfurl from their protective sheaths, or bracts.

Reedmace

Female catkin

Fluffy fruit

Bract

Style   *Petal*

Sepal

SEDGE SEEDS
In summer, the fuzzy yellowish flowerheads of false fox sedge (p.33) darken to ripe seeds, ready for dispersal along the pond bank.

Grey willow

Darkening seed head

PETALS AND SEPALS
The "petals" of the yellow flag are, in fact, made up of sepals, petals, and styles (the female parts of the flower that help to receive the pollen).

Cone

False fox sedge

Yellow flag

Marsh horsetail

CONE-BEARER
The marsh horsetail grows best in very moist ground and shallow water. Horsetails do not bear flowers. Instead, they have cone-like structures at their stem tips (compare with the marestail on p.12).

Early summer animals

EARLY SUMMER IS A TIME OF THINNING OUT and fattening up for pond animals. The swarms of young tadpoles, insect larvae, and water snails feed greedily on the abundant plant growth of this season (pp.10–11). But they are gradually thinned out by larger predatory creatures, such as beetle larvae and dragonfly nymphs (p.48), newts, and small fish. These grow fat, and in their turn they may fall prey to larger carnivores, from frogs, to fish such as carp and tench, to visiting birds like herons, and perhaps to water shrew, mink, and other mammals. And so the food chain of the pond builds up from plants to herbivores (plant-eaters), then to carnivores (meat-eaters). But this is not the end. Death comes to all and, when it does, creatures such as water slaters move in to eat the plant and animal remains. The droppings of all creatures enrich the water, providing minerals and other raw materials for fresh plant growth. So the nutrients go round and round, being recycled in the miniature ecosystem that is the pond.

Silver water beetle, wing cases lifted to show wings

Common toad

GOODBYE FOR THIS YEAR
A few of the dozens of breeding toads may still be lingering near the pond. But most have now dispersed to their favourite damp corners, such as in hedges, under logs, and among the undergrowth. They will not return to the pond until next spring.

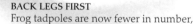

Tadpoles with developing hindlimbs

PETAL-LESS FLOWERS
Marestail is a shallow-water plant of ponds and streams, around whose stems squirm and swim the numerous tiny summer pond creatures. It bears tiny flowers without petals, where the leaves join the stem.

BACK LEGS FIRST
Frog tadpoles are now fewer in number, since many of their siblings have fallen prey to fish, newts, diving beetles, and dragonfly nymphs. They now have back legs, which appeared after about seven weeks. This change in body shape, from tadpole to adult frog, is called metamorphosis.

Great pond snail

GROWN UP
This great pond snail is nearing full size, at about 5 cm (2 in) long. It slides slowly over the bottom of the pond, eating decaying plant remains.

Marestail

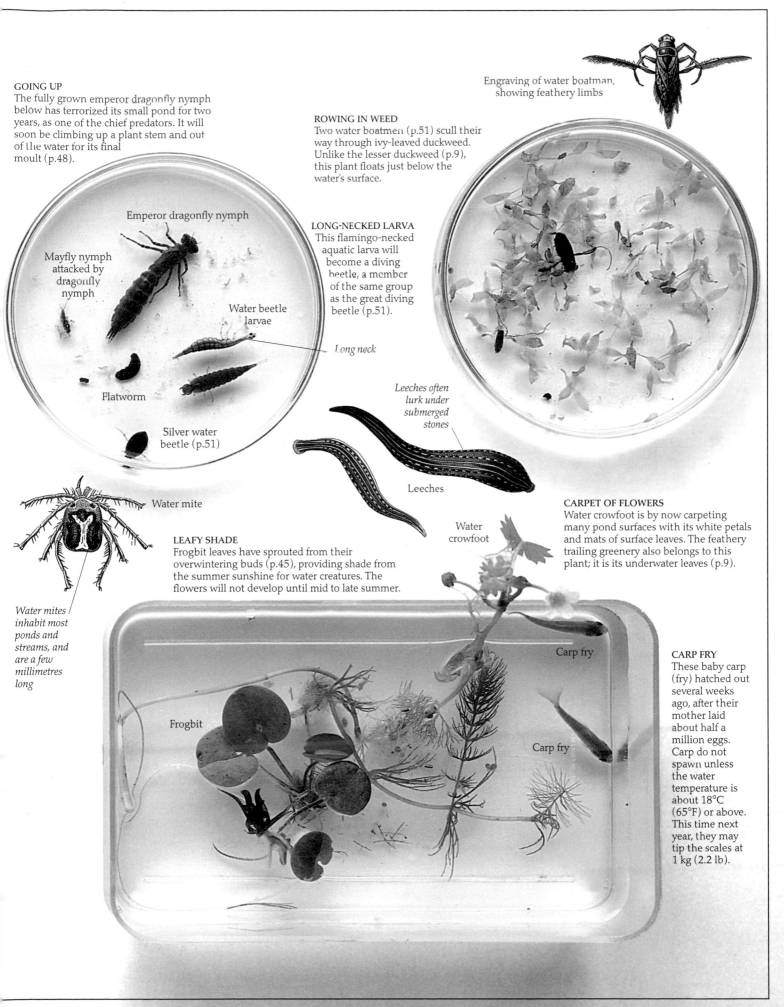

GOING UP
The fully grown emperor dragonfly nymph below has terrorized its small pond for two years, as one of the chief predators. It will soon be climbing up a plant stem and out of the water for its final moult (p.48).

Emperor dragonfly nymph

Mayfly nymph attacked by dragonfly nymph

Water beetle larvae

Flatworm

Silver water beetle (p.51)

Water mite

Water mites inhabit most ponds and streams, and are a few millimetres long

Engraving of water boatman, showing feathery limbs

ROWING IN WEED
Two water boatmen (p.51) scull their way through ivy-leaved duckweed. Unlike the lesser duckweed (p.9), this plant floats just below the water's surface.

LONG-NECKED LARVA
This flamingo-necked aquatic larva will become a diving beetle, a member of the same group as the great diving beetle (p.51).

Long neck

Leeches often lurk under submerged stones

Leeches

Water crowfoot

LEAFY SHADE
Frogbit leaves have sprouted from their overwintering buds (p.45), providing shade from the summer sunshine for water creatures. The flowers will not develop until mid to late summer.

CARPET OF FLOWERS
Water crowfoot is by now carpeting many pond surfaces with its white petals and mats of surface leaves. The feathery trailing greenery also belongs to this plant; it is its underwater leaves (p.9).

Frogbit

Carp fry

Carp fry

CARP FRY
These baby carp (fry) hatched out several weeks ago, after their mother laid about half a million eggs. Carp do not spawn unless the water temperature is about 18°C (65°F) or above. This time next year, they may tip the scales at 1 kg (2.2 lb).

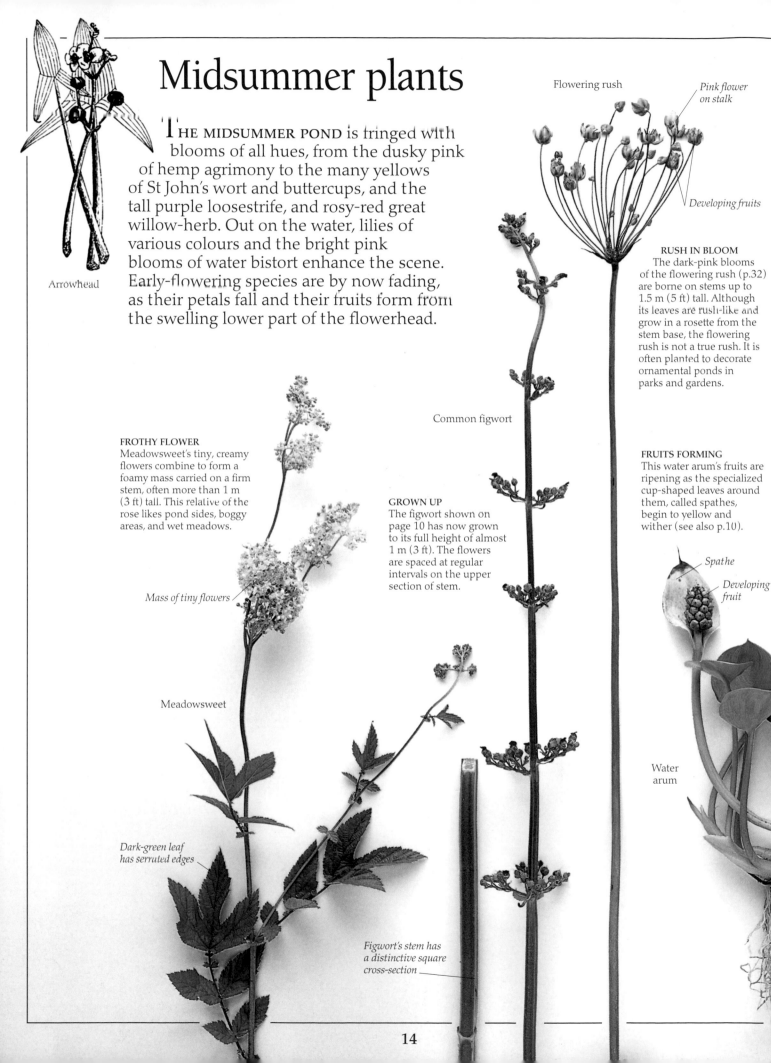

Midsummer plants

THE MIDSUMMER POND is fringed with blooms of all hues, from the dusky pink of hemp agrimony to the many yellows of St John's wort and buttercups, and the tall purple loosestrife, and rosy-red great willow-herb. Out on the water, lilies of various colours and the bright pink blooms of water bistort enhance the scene. Early-flowering species are by now fading, as their petals fall and their fruits form from the swelling lower part of the flowerhead.

Arrowhead

Flowering rush

Pink flower on stalk

Developing fruits

RUSH IN BLOOM
The dark-pink blooms of the flowering rush (p.32) are borne on stems up to 1.5 m (5 ft) tall. Although its leaves are rush-like and grow in a rosette from the stem base, the flowering rush is not a true rush. It is often planted to decorate ornamental ponds in parks and gardens.

Common figwort

FROTHY FLOWER
Meadowsweet's tiny, creamy flowers combine to form a foamy mass carried on a firm stem, often more than 1 m (3 ft) tall. This relative of the rose likes pond sides, boggy areas, and wet meadows.

Mass of tiny flowers

GROWN UP
The figwort shown on page 10 has now grown to its full height of almost 1 m (3 ft). The flowers are spaced at regular intervals on the upper section of stem.

FRUITS FORMING
This water arum's fruits are ripening as the specialized cup-shaped leaves around them, called spathes, begin to yellow and wither (see also p.10).

Spathe

Developing fruit

Meadowsweet

Water arum

Dark-green leaf has serrated edges

Figwort's stem has a distinctive square cross-section

GREYISH-GREEN SHEEN
Osier, a typically water-loving willow, has extremely long, sharply pointed leaves. The tiny hairs on the underside of each leaf give it a greyish green sheen.

Osier

Hawthorn

Haw

TALL SPRAYS
Water plantain's small, pinky-white flowers bloom on tall, erect sprays of stems at this time of year (p.57).

Leaf has a dark-green upperside

Underside of leaf is grey

GREEN TO RED
The hawthorn can tolerate wide variations in soil type and moisture content, so this tree is often found growing by ponds. The green fruits are called haws. In a few weeks, the haws will turn a deep, rich red colour and attract birds such as waxwings and tits to the pondside.

WITHERED PETALS
The bright blooms (p.11) of the yellow flag iris have withered to brown, and the fruit capsules are now forming. Each capsule resembles a chunky pea pod, and contains several knobbly seeds (p.4).

Seed pods

ST JOHN'S WORT
This plant (see also p.16) grows in damp places such as shady woods and pond banks. The flowers begin to fade in midsummer.

SPHERES AND SPEARS
The yellow flower of the greater spearwort indicates that this plant is a type of buttercup. Two spherical, spiky heads of ripening fruits can be seen here, as well as the spearshaped leaves that give the plant its name.

Withered flower

St John's wort

Ripening fruit

Yellow flag

PINK FORGET-ME-NOT
Water forget-me-not flowers throughout the summer in damp and shady places. Its stems trail along the pond edge, and its flowers may be blue, white, or pink.

Spear-shaped leaf

Water forget-me-not

Greater spearwort

Midsummer animals

MIDSUMMER IS A TIME OF GROWTH and departure in the pond. The frantic spring and early summer rush of new life is quietening. The surviving youngsters of this year's eggs, now fewer in number, settle down to the serious business of growing, laying down food stores, and preparing for the shorter, colder days ahead. Frog and toad tadpoles have transformed into air-breathing miniature adults, ready to leave the water and take their first hops on land. A few young newts may keep their gills and stay in tadpole form through the coming autumn and winter, but others, now adult in shape, are moving away. The exodus from the pond continues as aquatic insect larvae of many kinds develop into adults (p.50), from tiny gnats, midges, and mosquitoes to the mighty dragonflies (p.48) that prey on them.

Tiny gnats (male and female) dancing above the pond's surface on a summer evening

Water snail

Growth rings

RINGS AND BANDS
Periods of slow growth are visible on this water snail's shell. They are the thin rings towards the opening that cross the spiral banding pattern.

HAPPY WANDERER
The wandering snail tolerates a wider range of water conditions than the great pond snail and many other species, so it is more widespread in ponds and slow-moving rivers.

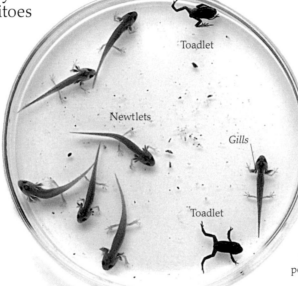

Toadlet

Newtlets

Gills

Toadlet

FLYING ROWER
This water boatman has opened its strong wings (p.51).

NEWTLETS
The young newts in this sample of pond water still retain their gills, to help absorb oxygen from the warm summer pond water. They hide among weeds, eating water fleas and other tiny creatures.

TOADLETS
By now, toad tadpoles have grown their front legs and lost their tails, so that they resemble their parents. In midsummer, they leave the pond for life on land.

SQUARE STEM
There are several species of St John's wort (p.15). This square-stemmed species lines watersides, marshes, and damp hedgerows.

Young freshwater molluscs

Wandering snails

Snail emerging from shell

BABY BIVALVES
In about 10 years, these young freshwater molluscs will grow to many times the size they are shown here (p.52). In their early years, they are busy feeding and absorbing calcium from the water to build their shell.

Square-stemmed St John's wort

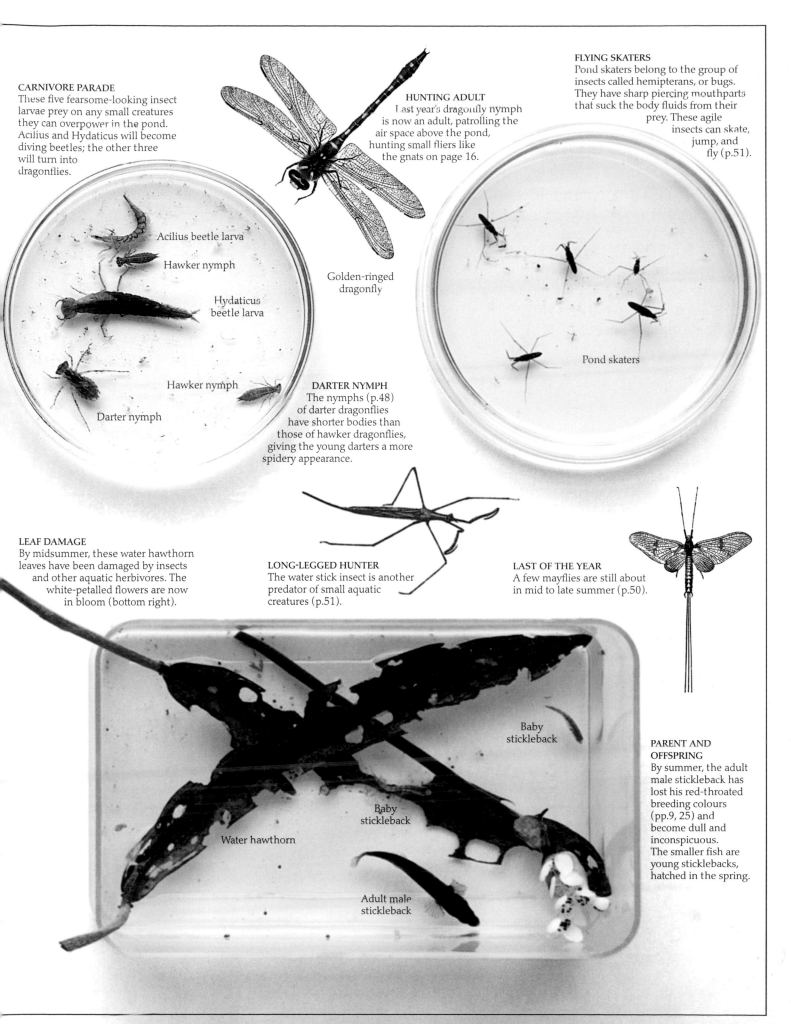

CARNIVORE PARADE
These five fearsome-looking insect larvae prey on any small creatures they can overpower in the pond. Acilius and Hydaticus will become diving beetles; the other three will turn into dragonflies.

Acilius beetle larva

Hawker nymph

Hydaticus beetle larva

Hawker nymph

Darter nymph

HUNTING ADULT
Last year's dragonfly nymph is now an adult, patrolling the air space above the pond, hunting small fliers like the gnats on page 16.

Golden-ringed dragonfly

FLYING SKATERS
Pond skaters belong to the group of insects called hemipterans, or bugs. They have sharp piercing mouthparts that suck the body fluids from their prey. These agile insects can skate, jump, and fly (p.51).

Pond skaters

DARTER NYMPH
The nymphs (p.48) of darter dragonflies have shorter bodies than those of hawker dragonflies, giving the young darters a more spidery appearance.

LEAF DAMAGE
By midsummer, these water hawthorn leaves have been damaged by insects and other aquatic herbivores. The white-petalled flowers are now in bloom (bottom right).

LONG-LEGGED HUNTER
The water stick insect is another predator of small aquatic creatures (p.51).

LAST OF THE YEAR
A few mayflies are still about in mid to late summer (p.50).

Baby stickleback

Baby stickleback

Water hawthorn

Adult male stickleback

PARENT AND OFFSPRING
By summer, the adult male stickleback has lost his red-throated breeding colours (pp.9, 25) and become dull and inconspicuous. The smaller fish are young sticklebacks, hatched in the spring.

The pond in autumn

GRADUALLY THE SUN'S ARC flattens across the sky, and the hours of daylight shorten. Although the rays may still be warm in midafternoon, the nights are becoming increasingly chilly. Autumn has arrived, and pond wildlife is slowing down and preparing for winter. Summer-visiting birds have departed, but their place will soon be taken by waterfowl such as the Brent goose, Bewick swan, and pintail duck (p.29), that fly in from their far-north breeding grounds to enliven larger ponds, lakes, and marshes. Mammals and resident birds feed greedily on the ripe fruits, building up their fat stores for the winter. However, their shelters and hiding places are gradually being whittled away, as the cold wind rattles crackly brown leaves from their stems, making the pond's banks look bare and untidy.

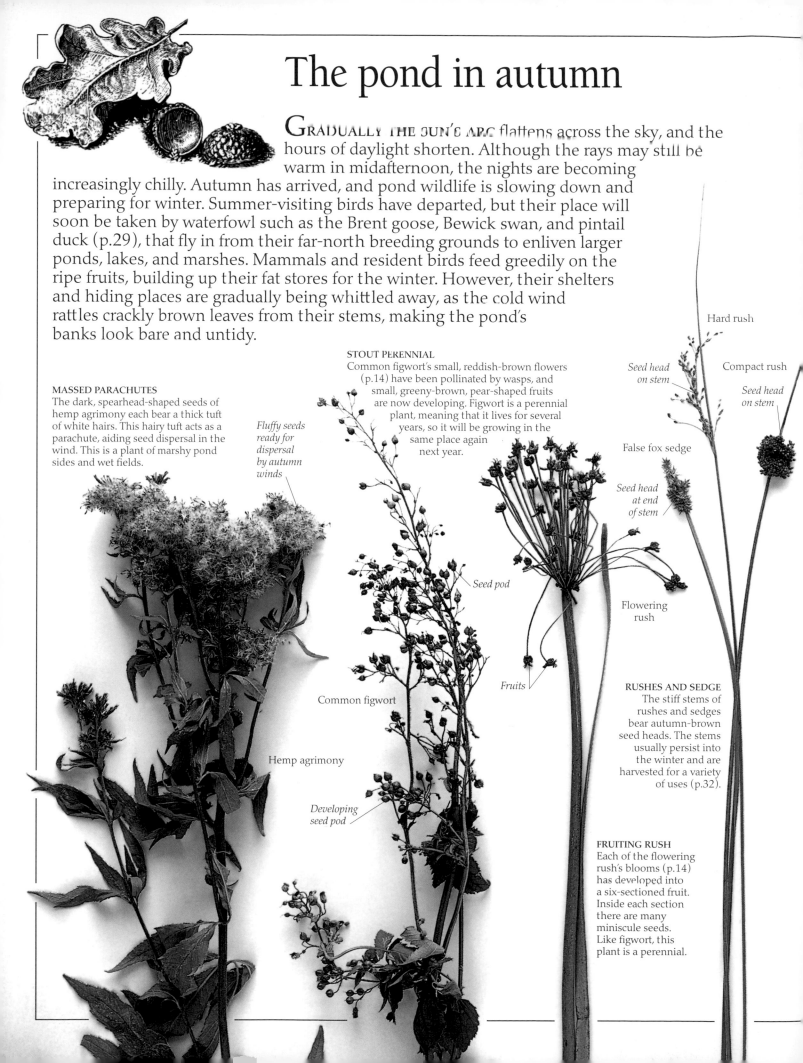

MASSED PARACHUTES
The dark, spearhead-shaped seeds of hemp agrimony each bear a thick tuft of white hairs. This hairy tuft acts as a parachute, aiding seed dispersal in the wind. This is a plant of marshy pond sides and wet fields.

Fluffy seeds ready for dispersal by autumn winds

STOUT PERENNIAL
Common figwort's small, reddish-brown flowers (p.14) have been pollinated by wasps, and small, greeny-brown, pear-shaped fruits are now developing. Figwort is a perennial plant, meaning that it lives for several years, so it will be growing in the same place again next year.

Seed pod

Common figwort

Hemp agrimony

Developing seed pod

Fruits

Flowering rush

Hard rush

Seed head on stem

Compact rush

Seed head on stem

False fox sedge

Seed head at end of stem

RUSHES AND SEDGE
The stiff stems of rushes and sedges bear autumn-brown seed heads. The stems usually persist into the winter and are harvested for a variety of uses (p.32).

FRUITING RUSH
Each of the flowering rush's blooms (p.14) has developed into a six-sectioned fruit. Inside each section there are many miniscule seeds. Like figwort, this plant is a perennial.

WINTER POKER
Reedmace's familiar brown, poker-shaped seed head stands guard over marshes and ponds, usually throughout the winter. In spring, the poker bursts to scatter the fluffy-haired seeds.

Brown poker full of seeds

SNAILS SLOWING DOWN
Falling water temperatures mean that even pond snails begin to move about more slowly, tending to stay in deeper water.

Pond snails

Reedmace

Newtlet

Caddis-fly cases

Dragonfly nymph

Alder

ALDER CONES
In autumn, the alder's green fruits ripen to a browny-black colour and stay on the tree during winter. They are sometimes mistaken for small pine cones, but the alder is not a conifer. It prefers pond banks and streamsides, and its light seeds drop onto the water and float to new ground.

Alder cones

TUBE HOMES
These tubes, made out of rolled up leaf fragments, are the larval cases of the great red sedge, a type of caddis fly (p.50). The larvae will emerge as adult flies next year.

Seed pod

NEXT YEAR'S ADULT
Dragonfly nymphs found in the pond at this time of year will overwinter and emerge next year.

AUTUMN JUVENILE
A young common newt, still equipped with gills, will overwinter as a juvenile, and finish its transformation into an adult next year.

RECYCLING FUNGI
Animal and plant corpses are digested by fungi, and their nutrients are made available for recycling. Here, an old pondside tree has been attacked and weakened by bracket fungi.

Bracket fungi grow on the outside of the trunk

ON THE BOTTOM
Leaves, twigs, and other debris blow into the pond, or are washed in by heavy autumn rains. This accumulation of debris, overlying the mud of the pond bed, will shelter all manner of small water creatures during the winter months.

Bracket fungi on wood

SOON TO SET SEED
The seed capsules, or pods, of this yellow flag iris are now thick with ripening brown seeds (compare those above with the same pods on p.15). Eventually the fleshy capsule walls dry out and split into three boat-shaped segments; these peel back to release the seeds (p.4).

Oak leaf

Willow leaf

Birch leaf

Yellow flag

Willow twigs

The pond in winter

WHERE DO FLIES GO IN THE WINTER? More to the point, where do pond snails, flatworms, aquatic larvae, fish, amphibians, and other pond creatures go in the winter? There are several strategies for surviving the season of cold and ice. Cold-blooded animals can generally live in the coldest water, provided they are not trapped in solid ice. Fish and some aquatic insects, molluscs, and worms move to the deepest part of the pond, to avoid being frozen in ice. As the water cools, they do, too, and their bodies need less and less energy, so they can survive with hardly any food. Cold water holds more dissolved oxygen than warm water, and oxygen supplies are enriched by various types of waterweed, which can still carry out photosynthesis (pp.10, 46) using the meagre sunlight that penetrates the layer of ice. Coupled with the reduced needs of the inactive animals, this means there are sufficient supplies of oxygen for life, even when the pond's surface is iced over for days. Another strategy, adopted by many very small water creatures, is to lay eggs in the autumn; the adults then die, but the eggs hatch the next spring. Amphibians, such as frogs and toads, sleep through the winter in a sheltered place on land.

Water-lily leaf

LAST REMAINS
Water-lily and arrowhead leaves still bear their long, anchoring stems in winter, but the leaves are now browned, tattered, and torn by waves, wind, and frost.

POND SKATERS
While animals and plants overwinter below the pond's surface, humans may be active above.

Common reed

WINDBURNED REED
Common reed flowerheads stubbornly resist winter's gales and snowstorms. Even the leaves stay stuck to the stems, though the combined effects of frost and windblasting turn them to crinkly brown ribbons.

Arrowhead leaf

Old leaves are evidence of the trees that grow round the pond

BLANKETS OF LEAVES
Decay is slow in the icy water. Shed leaves settle in blanket-like layers, which protect and insulate the small creatures and the winter buds of plants sandwiched between them.

THIS YEAR, NEXT YEAR
The alder's greenery has now disappeared (p.19), leaving the woody cones to rattle on the bare twigs. However, renewed growth is already heralded by next year's smaller, paler developing catkins.

Alder

Next year's catkins developing

This year's cones

WINTER WEEPING
Slender, leafless willow twigs overhang the pond, rattling in the breeze and easily shedding snow to prevent them cracking under its weight.

Bittersweet

END OF THE SEASON
One of our seasonal markers, the yellow flag iris, is now a brown and tattered remnant of its former green-and-yellow glory. Only the leaves persist; but new life is just around the corner.

Weeping willow twig

Red berries are poisonous

A TOUCH OF SCARLET
Bittersweet trails through the bank vegetation, its bright red berries adding a touch of colour to the winter landscape. Beware its attraction, though – the berries of bittersweet are poisonous.

Yellow flag

Sheet of ice lifted from shallow pond

ICE IS NICE
Strangely, a blanket of ice is no bad thing for pond inhabitants. Ice is a good insulator so, while temperatures may plummet far below freezing in the winds above, down in the pond's depths the water is a bearable few degrees above freezing.

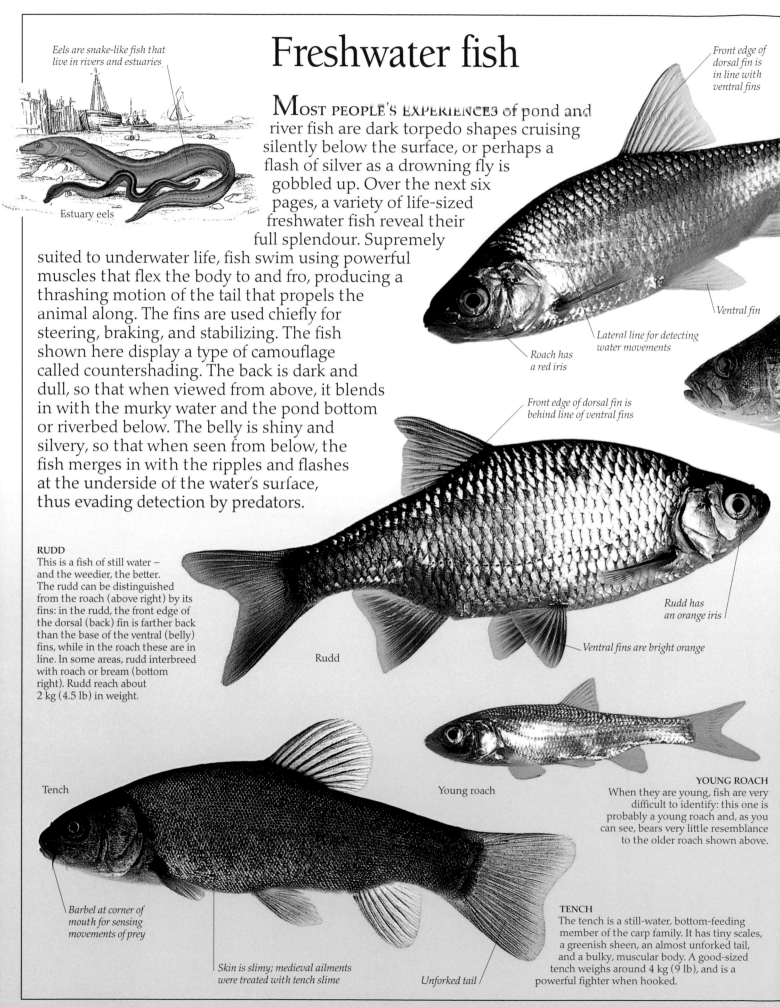

Eels are snake-like fish that live in rivers and estuaries

Estuary eels

Freshwater fish

MOST PEOPLE'S EXPERIENCES of pond and river fish are dark torpedo shapes cruising silently below the surface, or perhaps a flash of silver as a drowning fly is gobbled up. Over the next six pages, a variety of life-sized freshwater fish reveal their full splendour. Supremely suited to underwater life, fish swim using powerful muscles that flex the body to and fro, producing a thrashing motion of the tail that propels the animal along. The fins are used chiefly for steering, braking, and stabilizing. The fish shown here display a type of camouflage called countershading. The back is dark and dull, so that when viewed from above, it blends in with the murky water and the pond bottom or riverbed below. The belly is shiny and silvery, so that when seen from below, the fish merges in with the ripples and flashes at the underside of the water's surface, thus evading detection by predators.

Front edge of dorsal fin is in line with ventral fins

Ventral fin

Lateral line for detecting water movements

Roach has a red iris

Front edge of dorsal fin is behind line of ventral fins

RUDD
This is a fish of still water – and the weedier, the better. The rudd can be distinguished from the roach (above right) by its fins: in the rudd, the front edge of the dorsal (back) fin is farther back than the base of the ventral (belly) fins, while in the roach these are in line. In some areas, rudd interbreed with roach or bream (bottom right). Rudd reach about 2 kg (4.5 lb) in weight.

Rudd

Rudd has an orange iris

Ventral fins are bright orange

Tench

Young roach

YOUNG ROACH
When they are young, fish are very difficult to identify: this one is probably a young roach and, as you can see, bears very little resemblance to the older roach shown above.

Barbel at corner of mouth for sensing movements of prey

Skin is slimy; medieval ailments were treated with tench slime

Unforked tail

TENCH
The tench is a still-water, bottom-feeding member of the carp family. It has tiny scales, a greenish sheen, an almost unforked tail, and a bulky, muscular body. A good-sized tench weighs around 4 kg (9 lb), and is a powerful fighter when hooked.

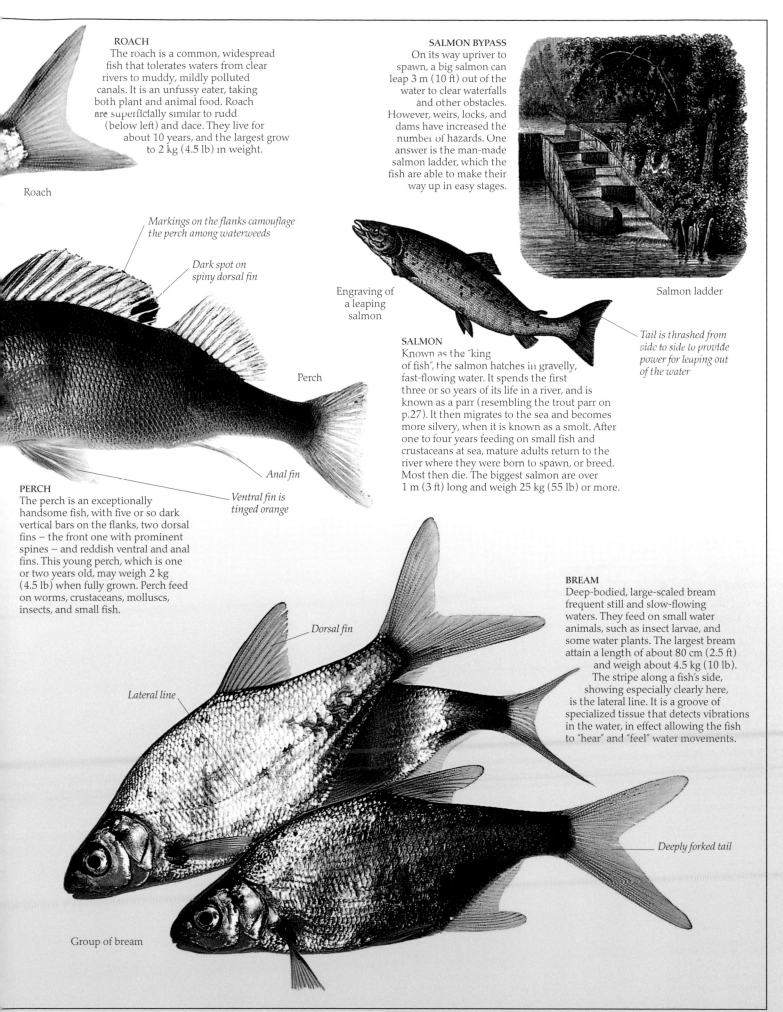

ROACH

The roach is a common, widespread fish that tolerates waters from clear rivers to muddy, mildly polluted canals. It is an unfussy eater, taking both plant and animal food. Roach are superficially similar to rudd (below left) and dace. They live for about 10 years, and the largest grow to 2 kg (4.5 lb) in weight.

Roach

SALMON BYPASS

On its way upriver to spawn, a big salmon can leap 3 m (10 ft) out of the water to clear waterfalls and other obstacles. However, weirs, locks, and dams have increased the number of hazards. One answer is the man-made salmon ladder, which the fish are able to make their way up in easy stages.

Salmon ladder

Markings on the flanks camouflage the perch among waterweeds

Dark spot on spiny dorsal fin

Engraving of a leaping salmon

SALMON

Known as the "king of fish", the salmon hatches in gravelly, fast-flowing water. It spends the first three or so years of its life in a river, and is known as a parr (resembling the trout parr on p.27). It then migrates to the sea and becomes more silvery, when it is known as a smolt. After one to four years feeding on small fish and crustaceans at sea, mature adults return to the river where they were born to spawn, or breed. Most then die. The biggest salmon are over 1 m (3 ft) long and weigh 25 kg (55 lb) or more.

Perch

Tail is thrashed from side to side to provide power for leaping out of the water

Anal fin

Ventral fin is tinged orange

PERCH

The perch is an exceptionally handsome fish, with five or so dark vertical bars on the flanks, two dorsal fins – the front one with prominent spines – and reddish ventral and anal fins. This young perch, which is one or two years old, may weigh 2 kg (4.5 lb) when fully grown. Perch feed on worms, crustaceans, molluscs, insects, and small fish.

Dorsal fin

Lateral line

BREAM

Deep-bodied, large-scaled bream frequent still and slow-flowing waters. They feed on small water animals, such as insect larvae, and some water plants. The largest bream attain a length of about 80 cm (2.5 ft) and weigh about 4.5 kg (10 lb). The stripe along a fish's side, showing especially clearly here, is the lateral line. It is a groove of specialized tissue that detects vibrations in the water, in effect allowing the fish to "hear" and "feel" water movements.

Deeply forked tail

Group of bream

23

Continued on next page

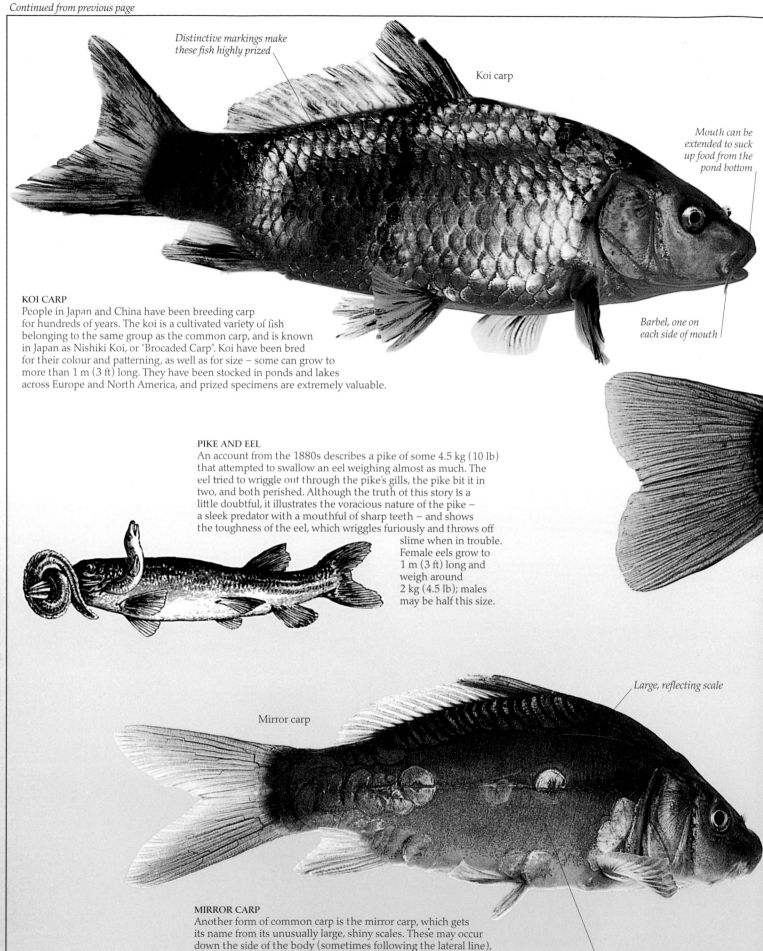

Distinctive markings make these fish highly prized

Koi carp

Mouth can be extended to suck up food from the pond bottom

Barbel, one on each side of mouth

KOI CARP

People in Japan and China have been breeding carp for hundreds of years. The koi is a cultivated variety of fish belonging to the same group as the common carp, and is known in Japan as Nishiki Koi, or "Brocaded Carp". Koi have been bred for their colour and patterning, as well as for size – some can grow to more than 1 m (3 ft) long. They have been stocked in ponds and lakes across Europe and North America, and prized specimens are extremely valuable.

PIKE AND EEL

An account from the 1880s describes a pike of some 4.5 kg (10 lb) that attempted to swallow an eel weighing almost as much. The eel tried to wriggle out through the pike's gills, the pike bit it in two, and both perished. Although the truth of this story is a little doubtful, it illustrates the voracious nature of the pike – a sleek predator with a mouthful of sharp teeth – and shows the toughness of the eel, which wriggles furiously and throws off slime when in trouble. Female eels grow to 1 m (3 ft) long and weigh around 2 kg (4.5 lb); males may be half this size.

Large, reflecting scale

Mirror carp

MIRROR CARP

Another form of common carp is the mirror carp, which gets its name from its unusually large, shiny scales. These may occur down the side of the body (sometimes following the lateral line), and perhaps along the back, or scattered at random. Like other carp, it feeds on the bottom, consuming small aquatic creatures and water plants. It reaches weights of up to 9 kg (20 lb).

Parts of the body have no scales

*Blue flash identifies
the fish as a bitterling*

Short lateral line

Bitterling

BITTERLING
Resembling a miniature crucian carp in shape, the bitterling is an attractive little fish that is fully grown at about 8 cm (3 in) long. It lives in ponds, lakes, and slow rivers, eating small water creatures and plants. It has a unique method of spawning. In late spring, the female develops a long tube, through which she lays her eggs in a freshwater mussel such as a swan mussel (p.52). The male deposits his sperm nearby, which are sucked in by the mussel and fertilize the eggs. The eggs develop and hatch inside the mussel, and young fry leave their host after about three weeks, when their yolk sacs have been exhausted.

STICKLEBACK NEST
The male stickleback makes a nest of plant material in late spring. He does a zig-zag dance to attract a female, who lays her eggs in the nest. He fertilizes them, and the next day entices another female. After several egg batches have been laid, the male guards them until they hatch.

*Adult has a
very deep body*

*Overlapping scales can be golden,
bronze, or olive-green*

Crucian carp

CRUCIAN CARP
A relative of the common carp, the crucian is even more tolerant of water that is low in dissolved oxygen. This fish inhabits weedy, stagnating ponds and lakes, canals, reservoirs, and slow rivers. An average adult is 30 cm (1 ft) long and weighs 250 g (10 oz), although record-breakers of more than 2 kg (4.5 lb) have been caught. The crucian has a deeper body than the common carp, and it lacks the small feelers called barbels on the side of the mouth.

Grass carp

GRASS CARP
This plant-eating, golden-coloured fish is a native of China and Russia, and it has been introduced into waterways in other countries to control weed growth. In its native habitat, the grass carp can reach up to 35 kg (75 lb) in weight, although introduced specimens are usually around 4 kg (9 lb).

*Barbels on
mouth*

*Spots on dorsal
side (back)*

GUDGEON
The carnivorous gudgeon grubs about on the bottom using its two barbels to locate food such as worms, insect larvae, and other small water creatures. It rarely grows to more than 15 cm (6 in) long. Shoals of gudgeon are common in rivers, especially in the middle sections; they can also be found in lakes and canals.

Speckled, translucent fins

Gudgeon

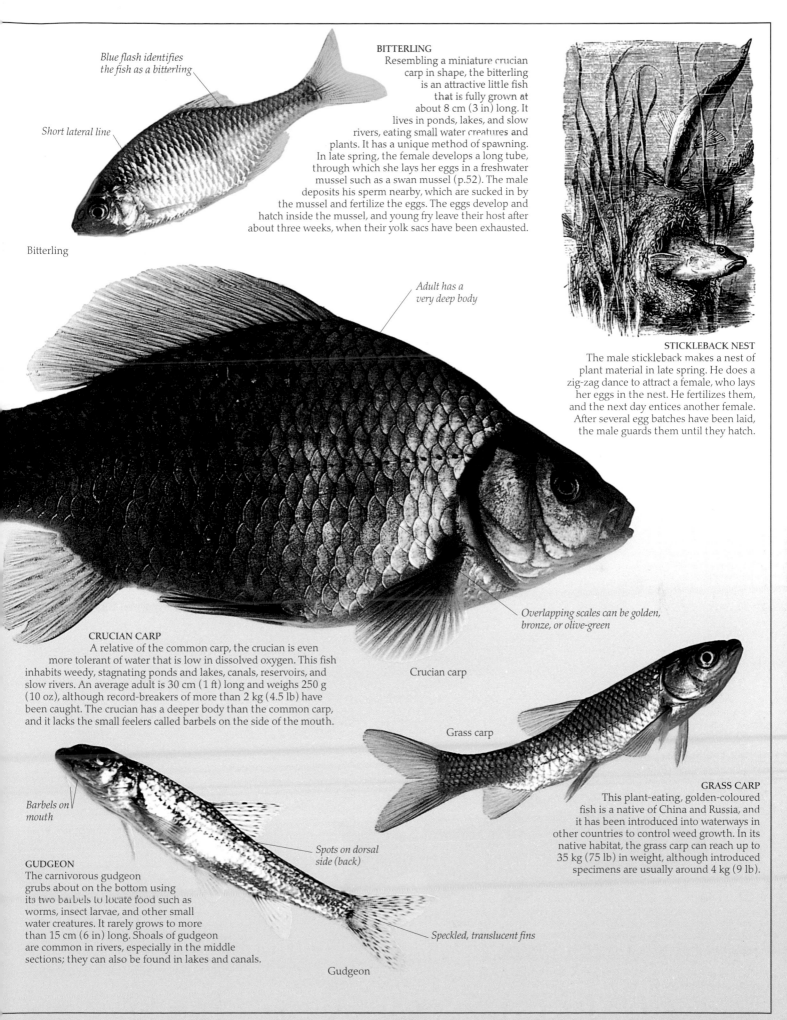

The trout

Few freshwater fish match the trout for natural beauty and grace, for fighting power when hooked – and for taste when cooked! Trout belong to the salmon family. The brown trout and sea trout are, in fact, different forms of the same species. The former lives all its life in fresh water; the latter feeds in the sea and enters its home stream in summer, to breed in autumn. Adult brown trout may approach 1 m (3 ft) in length, while sea trout can be half as long again. There are many intermediates between these two forms, and distinguishing between them is difficult, as sea trout darken when they have been in fresh water for a few weeks and resemble the brown trout. In any case, trout vary enormously in appearance, depending on where they live, the nature of the water, the type of stream or lake bed, and the food they eat. Rainbow trout are another trout species altogether.

TYPICAL TROUT COUNTRY
An ideal trout stream has clear and cool running water with high levels of dissolved oxygen, and a gravelly bed for spawning. Trout are also found in clean lakes, usually in the shallows near their food.

Lateral line

Movements of the very mobile pectoral fins enable the fish to swim upwards or downwards

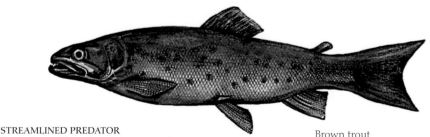

STREAMLINED PREDATOR
Brown trout, like other trout, are carnivorous. Food varies from tiny water fleas, flies, aquatic insect larvae (such as caddis-fly larvae), and freshwater shrimps, to shellfish and other molluscs. The big ferox brown trout, from large, deep lakes, prey on other fish, including char and whitefish.

Brown trout

COLOURS OF THE RAINBOW
Rainbow trout were originally found in western North America (especially California). Like the brown trout, there are sea, lake, and river forms. Their eggs were brought to Europe in the 1910s, and these fish have since been introduced into many rivers, reservoirs, and lakes, to provide sport for anglers as well as food. Rainbow trout breed in some large reservoirs, but rivers have to be regularly stocked with young fish produced on trout farms. Rainbow trout can live in warmer, less oxygenated water than the brown trout, so they are stocked in small lakes and large ponds; brown trout would probably not survive in such small bodies of water.

8 days: eggs are
mostly yolk

21 days: eye spots and
backbones are visible

28 days: head and body
shapes are distinguishable,
curled within eggs

35 days: alevins (larvae)
hatch, still attached
to yolk sacs

TROUT DEVELOPMENT

The female trout lays her eggs in gravel,
and the male fertilizes them with a milky
fluid called milt, which contains sperm.
Trout eggs are 3–5 mm (0.12–0.2 in)
in diameter, and at first they are full
of yellow yolk. Within three weeks,
at hatchery temperatures, the dark eye
spots are visible. The larvae, called
alevins, emerge at five weeks.

*Distinctive flank markings
resemble thumb prints*

RAINBOW TROUT PARR

Trout alevins develop
through the fry stage (less
than one year old) into
young, but immature, fish
called parr. They grow fast if food is
plentiful, and on a trout farm they can
reach almost 4 kg (9 lb) in as many years.
The fish are ready to breed after two or three
years. Selective breeding is producing larger
and larger strains of rainbow trout.

Rainbow trout parr

*Iridescent stripe
along flank*

Dorsal fin

Small black dots along back

Adipose fin

*Rainbow trout have
spots on their tails;
brown trout do not*

*Ventral fin
(also known as
the pelvic fin)*

Silver belly

Anal fin

Two-year-old rainbow trout

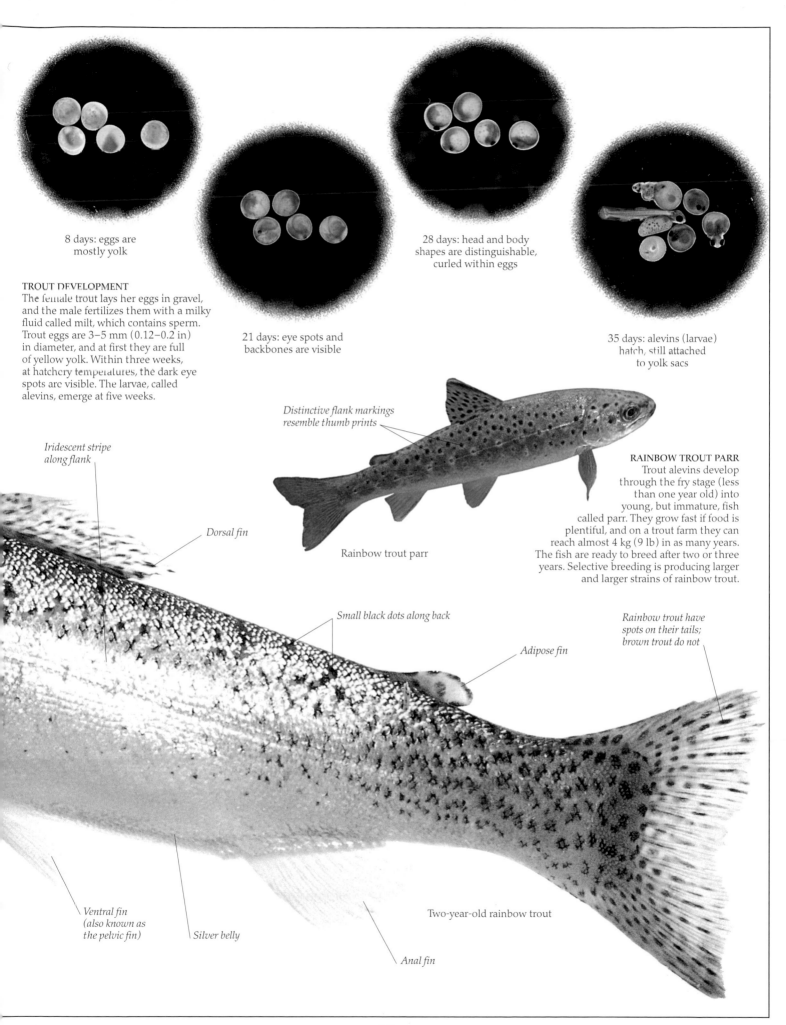

Waterfowl

WATER AND ITS RESIDENT WILDLIFE attract an amazing variety of birds. Quite at home on ponds, lakes, and rivers (as well as seashores) across the world are about 150 species of wildfowl, including swans, geese, and ducks. These generally heavy-bodied birds have webbed feet for swimming, and long, mobile necks for dabbling in the water and rummaging in the muddy bed for food. During spring, the dense bank vegetation provides many species with safe and sheltered nesting sites. In summer, the proud parents can be seen leading their fluffy chicks across the water. Aquatic plants and animals are a ready source of food for most of the year. In winter, when ponds freeze over, many wildfowl retreat to parks and gardens, where they feast on scraps donated by well-wishing humans. Others fly south, often covering vast distances to find a more favourable climate in which to spend the winter.

Teal nest and eggs

Eider duck nest and eggs

Soft down feathers insulate the eggs in the nest

SPECIALLY GROWN DOWN
Ultra-soft eiderdown feathers grow on the female eider duck's breast. She plucks them to cocoon her eggs as she nests on the seashore, lake side, or riverbank.

TEAL NEST
The teal makes its nest in dense undergrowth. The female is very careful when visiting her chicks, so as not to attract predators.

TUFTED DUCK EGG
A female tufted duck lays 6–14 eggs in a nest close to the water's edge. The chicks hatch after about 25 days in the eggs, and within a day they are swimming.

Teal, one of the
smallest ducks

*Nest would be
lined with down
when being used*

After the breeding season,
the male pintail (below)
moults to an inconspicuous
plumage, called eclipse plumage,
resembling the female's colouring.

Pintail
wing

MALE AND FEMALE
In the breeding
season, most male
ducks, like the pintail
(far right), have bright
plumage to catch the
female's eye. The female
(right) is duller, for
camouflage on the nest.

Tufted duck

PARTIAL TO MUSSELS
The tufted duck feeds on freshwater
mussels, as well as small fish, frogs,
and insects.

Tufted
duck skull

ON THE WING
Like other wildfowl,
pintail ducks are strong
fliers, many covering
vast distances during
their annual migration.

MUSCOVY DUCK
This native of Central and South
American ponds and marshes has
a broad bill that takes aquatic
plants and animals alike.

Muscovy duck

Muscovy
duck skull

BEWARE THE ORANGE BILL
The mute swan's bill is normally covered by an
orange sheath. Male swans can be extremely
vicious, particularly when defending their
territory during the breeding season.

Mute
swan

Vane

*Broad bill shape is
ideal for dabbling
for water
vegetation*

Quill

FROM THE MOULT
Waterfowl depend on
their feathers to keep them
dry, so they spend a lot of
time preening to keep the
feathers in good condition.

Mute swan skull

Flight feathers

Waterbirds

A STRETCH OF WATER acts as a magnet for all types of bird life. Many species, from sparrows to pheasants, come to drink. Others come to feed, from the tall, elegant heron that stands motionless as it watches for prey, to the flash of shimmering blue that signifies a kingfisher diving for its dinner. Bank plants, floating and submerged waterweeds, fish, frogs, insect larvae, shellfish, and other aquatic life provide food for many birds. Some species, like reed buntings and warblers, find security in the impenetrable reed beds and dense waterside vegetation. Here, they nest and raise their chicks, safe from predators such as foxes and hawks.

Kingfisher wing

Kingfisher

The white eggs have a glossy surface

THE EXPERT ANGLER
The brilliantly coloured kingfisher dives from its favourite perch for fish, tadpoles, and shellfish. The broadsword-shaped bill is ideal for stabbing or spearing fish, then holding the slippery prey until it can be beaten into stillness on a branch and swallowed headfirst.

Kingfisher eggs

WHITE EGGS
Kingfishers nest in a stream bank burrow up to 1 m (3 ft) long. Their eggs are white, since there is no need for camouflaging colours in the nest.

KINGFISHER WING AND TAIL
The electric colours act as a warning to predatory birds, advertizing that the flesh is foul-tasting.

Tail and wing markings vary from species to species

Kingfisher tail

Short wings beat rapidly in flight

Kingfisher skull

Sharp bill for stabbing fish

Long, sharp bill for spearing fish

Heron skull

Heron

LONG AND LANKY
Herons inhabit ponds, marshes, and rivers, stalking fish and frogs in the shallows.

HERON'S HARPOON
The heron's fearsome bill makes an excellent fish-stabbing spear. This bird stands patiently until prey comes within reach, then darts out its long neck, stabs the victim, tosses it round, and swallows it whole.

Bittern skull

BITTERN
This bird points its bill skywards and sways with the reeds to avoid detection. It can also climb up reed stems. The bittern builds a shallow platform of reed leaves and stalks, hidden deep in the reed beds. Its five to six eggs take four weeks to hatch.

STEALTHY STALKER
The bittern is a solitary, daytime feeder that uses its pointed bill to catch frogs, small fish, and insects.

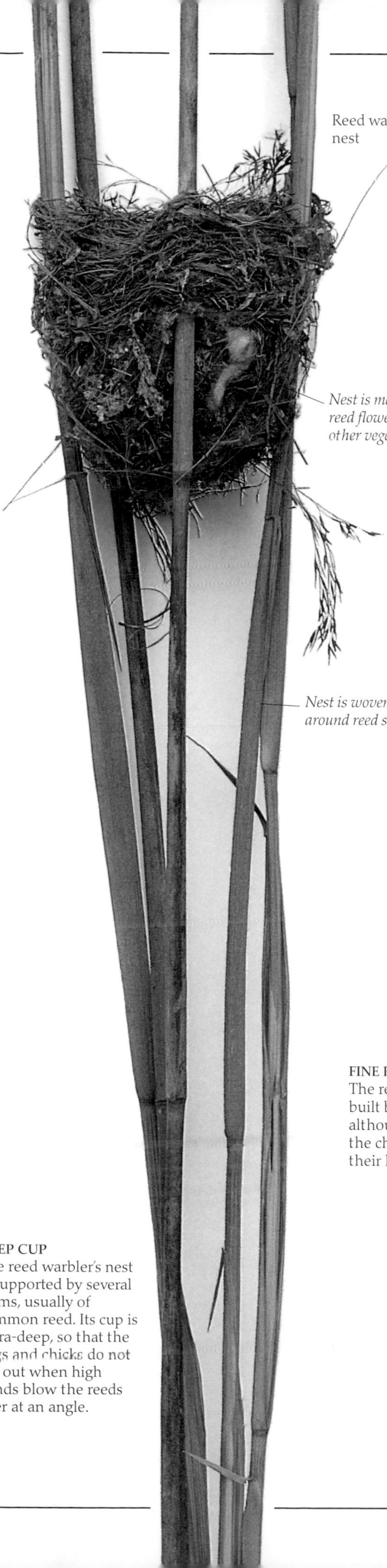

Reed warbler nest

Nest is made from reed flowerheads and other vegetation

Nest is woven around reed stalks

Reed warbler

☞ WARNING
All the eggs shown here come from established museum collections. Collecting or handling wild birds' eggs is now illegal. ☜

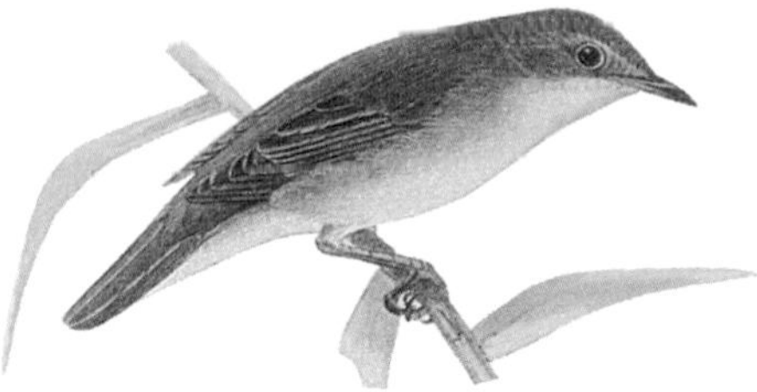

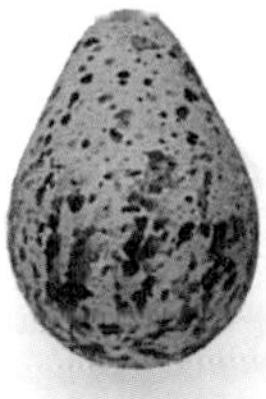

SNIPE EGG
The eggs of this small wading bird have camouflage colouring to hide them in the nest.

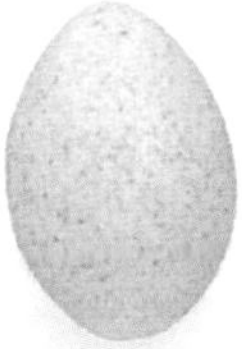

LITTLE GREBE EGG
White when laid, the little grebe's eggs get discoloured by plants and mud. The little grebe is also known as the dabchick.

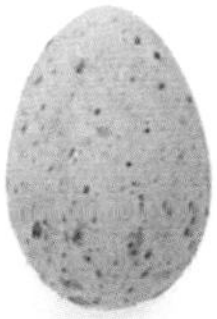

WATER RAIL EGG
Water rails are shy birds of the waterside undergrowth. There can be as many as 15 eggs in a clutch.

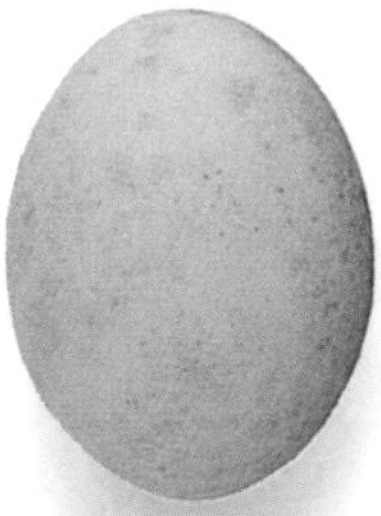

HERON EGG
The blue eggs are laid in well-defended nests built of sticks and twigs.

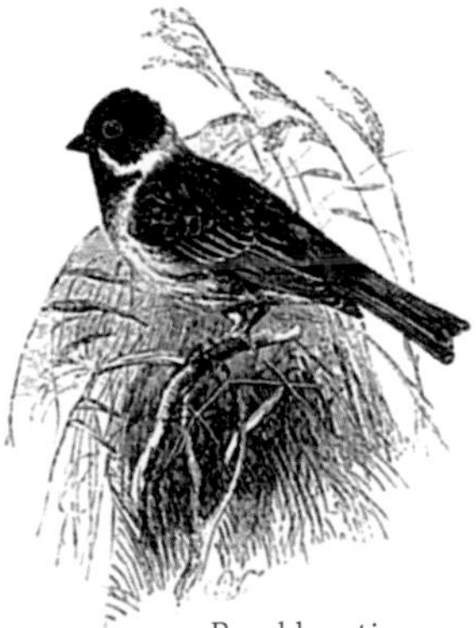

Reed bunting

FINE RUSHWORK
The reed bunting's nest is built by the female alone, although both parents feed the chicks on insects and their larvae.

Nest is made of grasses and moss

Reed bunting nest

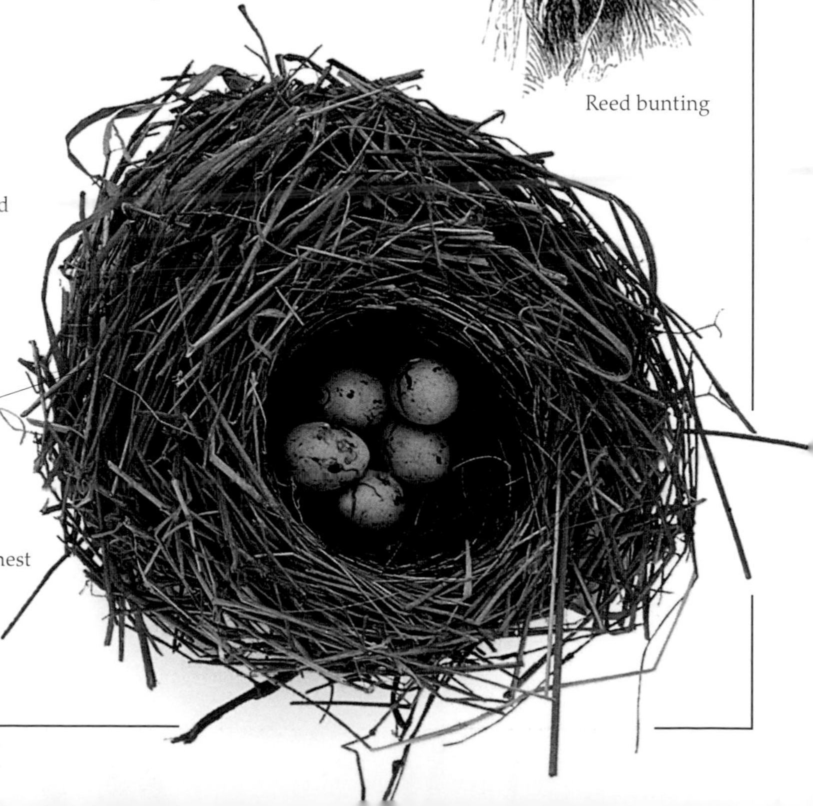

DEEP CUP
The reed warbler's nest is supported by several stems, usually of common reed. Its cup is extra-deep, so that the eggs and chicks do not fall out when high winds blow the reeds over at an angle.

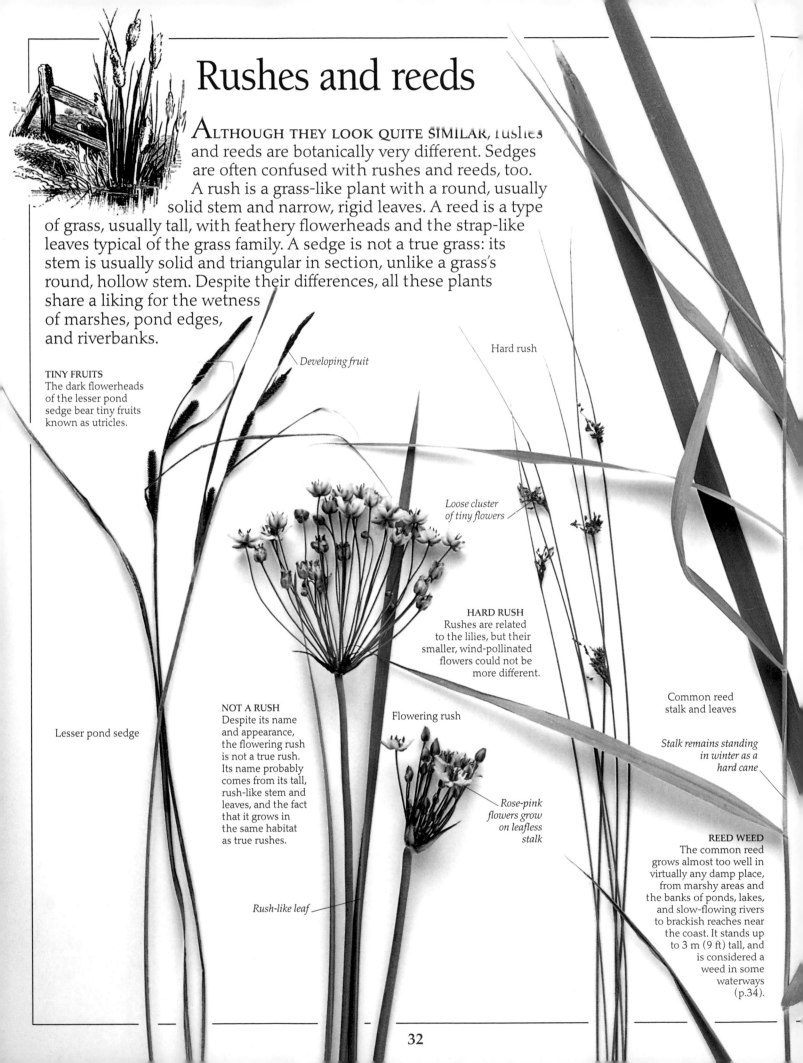

Rushes and reeds

ALTHOUGH THEY LOOK QUITE SIMILAR, rushes and reeds are botanically very different. Sedges are often confused with rushes and reeds, too. A rush is a grass-like plant with a round, usually solid stem and narrow, rigid leaves. A reed is a type of grass, usually tall, with feathery flowerheads and the strap-like leaves typical of the grass family. A sedge is not a true grass: its stem is usually solid and triangular in section, unlike a grass's round, hollow stem. Despite their differences, all these plants share a liking for the wetness of marshes, pond edges, and riverbanks.

Developing fruit

Hard rush

TINY FRUITS
The dark flowerheads of the lesser pond sedge bear tiny fruits known as utricles.

Loose cluster of tiny flowers

HARD RUSH
Rushes are related to the lilies, but their smaller, wind-pollinated flowers could not be more different.

Lesser pond sedge

NOT A RUSH
Despite its name and appearance, the flowering rush is not a true rush. Its name probably comes from its tall, rush-like stem and leaves, and the fact that it grows in the same habitat as true rushes.

Flowering rush

Common reed stalk and leaves

Stalk remains standing in winter as a hard cane

Rose-pink flowers grow on leafless stalk

REED WEED
The common reed grows almost too well in virtually any damp place, from marshy areas and the banks of ponds, lakes, and slow-flowing rivers to brackish reaches near the coast. It stands up to 3 m (9 ft) tall, and is considered a weed in some waterways (p.34).

Rush-like leaf

Male flower releases clouds of pollen

Female flower is fertilized by wind-carried pollen from male flowers, and fluffy seeds are released when the flowerhead splits open

Great reedmace

False fox sedge

Two to four female flowerheads

Male and female flowers in the same flowerhead

Triangular stem has sharp edges if rubbed downwards

FALSE FOX SEDGE
On top of false fox sedge's sharp-edged stems sit the tufty, yellow-green flowerheads. These contain both male and female flowers.

TWO HEADS IN ONE
The poker-shaped flowerhead of the great reedmace is in two parts. Above are hundreds of golden pollen-bearing male organs, and below are thousands of tiny female flowers packed into the brown cigar-shape. The whole flowerhead resembles a mace, a weapon of medieval knights – hence the name. The plant is commonly, but wrongly, called the bulrush, after the painting of *Moses in the Bulrushes* (p.35).

10 to 20 male flowerheads

Branched bur-reed

BRANCHING OUT
Each stem of branched bur-reed bears both male and female flowers. The smaller, ball-shaped flowers towards the tip are male; the female flowers are larger and spiky, rather like a rolled-up hedgehog.

Branched bur-reed

Flower stalk

Bract (leafy flap) at base of each branch of flower stalk

The reed bed

THE REED BED IS THE SILENT INVADER OF OPEN WATER. Dense growths of tall, marshy-ground plants, such as reedmace and common reed, spread around the pond's edge by thick underground stems (rhizomes). These grow sideways through the mud towards the water and send up fresh shoots at intervals. They spread into the shallows, pushing aside water-lilies and marestails. The strong new reed stems slow any water movements and trap current-borne particles. At the end of each season the old leaves, stems, and fruits add to the accumulating tangle. Within a few years previously open water can be turned into thickly vegetated marsh. Some years later the reed bed has moved on, still swallowing up the shallows, and drier-ground plants such as osiers and sallows (types of willow) have moved in at the back of the bed. This conversion of water to land by characteristic stages is an example of what biologists call ecological succession.

WATER TO DRY LAND
Shown below are the characteristic plants of pond and lake edges, with sallows and sedges higher up the shore, reed beds towards the middle, and marestails and long-stemmed lilies in deeper water. As the reeds spread and invade the water, this becomes clogged and marshy, and over the years, the whole pattern of plant growth moves towards the centre of the pond. Of course, this does not happen in all bodies of water. People clear or harvest the reeds, while storms, flood currents, plant diseases, and feeding animals keep a natural balance.

A ROOF OF REEDS
Being strong and long-lasting, reeds are widely used for roofing, including on huts in Egypt and Sudan, houses on stilts in Indonesia, and wooden cabins in southern North America. The English thatch style (above) offers excellent rain-repelling and insulating features. A skilled thatcher working with high-quality reeds can make a roof that remains weatherproof for at least 40 years.

CREEPING CRESS
The fool's watercress gets its name because its leaves resemble true watercress. It is found in large quantities at the back of many reed beds, its horizontal, straggling stems adding to the general tangle of vegetation.

RICH MUD
The thick, black mud of the reed bed is rich in decaying plant and animal remains. Its nutrients are soon recycled by the rushes, reeds, and other plants.

Reed-bed mud

Fool's watercress

Sallows

Reed bed

Water-lilies

Dry land

Marshy area

Shallow water

Open water

Underground rhizome

Horizontal stems

Sweet flag

Long, straight stalk

Flowerhead may be 2.5 m (8 ft) above roots

Dark-greeen leaf has pale underside

EARLY HARVEST
The reed cutter's season is usually the tail-end of winter and early spring. Last year's stems are cut near the base, before this year's shoots emerge, thus ensuring a future harvest.

THICK AND FLESHY
The juicy, strap-shaped leaves of sweet flag sprout from a thick horizontal stem, which itself bears many small roots that help in the process of binding the glutinous marshy mud.

Osier shoot

The thin leaves dry quickly when picked

Top of common reed stem

MOSES IN THE ... ?
According to the Bible, when Moses was a baby he was hidden in a basket in a reed bed on the River Nile's banks to avoid detection. Illustrations showing this are usually titled *Moses in the Bulrushes*, although most versions actually portray the baby in a clump of reedmace. This confusion has led to the name "bulrush" being popularly but incorrectly applied to reedmace (p.33).

WILLOWS FOR WEAVING
Osiers are found at the back of reed beds, on less marshy ground. They have long, straight shoots and a shrubby shape. They are often coppiced (cut at ground level) to provide bendy stems called withies for weaving chairs and baskets.

THE STRAIGHT AND NARROW
The straight, narrow stems of common reed are ideal thatching material. They are also used to make paper and other pulp-based materials. Plant growth in reed beds is often relatively fast, with plenty of water and nutrients, and slender stems and leaves that allow light to penetrate to the lower levels.

Base of common reed stem

Waterside mammals

Freshwater habitats, from rivers and streams to the marshy edges of lakes and ponds, provide a home and food for a number of mammals. All the aquatic mammals shown here have fur coats adapted to their watery habitat. The fur of a mink, for example, is of two main types. Long, thick, flattened guard hairs provide physical protection and camouflaging colouration. For each guard hair there are 20 or more softer hairs of the underfur, only half as long, that trap air to keep water out and body heat in. The owners sensibly spend much time combing and cleaning their fur, keeping it in tip-top condition. Another adaptation for an aquatic life is webs between the toes, for more efficient swimming.

FURRY FORAGER
The water shrew's dark-furred body is only about 9 cm (3 in) long. This bustling insectivore often lives in a bankside system of narrow tunnels that press water from its coat as it squeezes through. In the water, shrews catch small fish, insects, and even frogs; on land they forage for worms and other small creatures.

Mink

Canine teeth *Molar teeth* American mink skull

ADAPTABLE CARNIVORE
Minks are less specialized hunters than otters. As well as fish, they will take birds, aquatic insects, and land animals such as rabbits. The mink's broad, webbed back feet provide the main swimming power.

TEARERS AND SHEARERS
The mink uses the four long canine teeth at the front of its mouth to catch prey and tear flesh. The ridged molar teeth at the back are for shearing meat.

Elongated bill for grinding food

Platypus skull

Platypus

SENSITIVE HUNTER
The Australian platypus is an egg-laying mammal, or monotreme. It has a duck-like bill covered with leathery, sensitive skin. The platypus closes its eyes and ears when diving, and uses its bill to detect food by touch as it forages in muddy creek beds.

TOOTHLESS JAWS
When a baby platypus hatches, it has teeth, but these are soon lost. Adults grind up their food of shellfish, water insects, and worms using horny plates along their jaws.

Beaver lodge

Mud-and-stick walls *Living chamber (above water)* *Dam*

LODGE IN THE RIVER
A beaver family lives in a semi-submerged mud-and-stick house called a lodge. The beavers build a dam of branches, twigs, stones, and mud across a river or stream, which raises the local water level and isolates the lodge for safety. During winter, they swim under the ice to a "deep freezer" food cache of woody stems and twigs.

Entrance (under water) *Food store* *Raised water level*

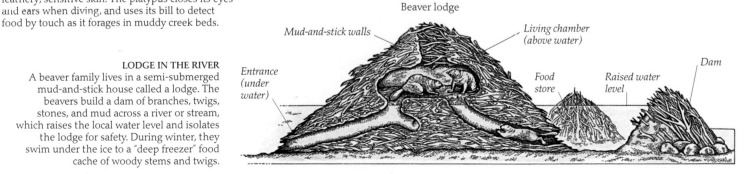

Long canine teeth for grasping fish

Otter skull

EYES ON TOP
An otter's nostrils, eyes, and ears are high on its head, so that the otter can swim almost submerged yet still breathe, look, and listen.

HUNTING THE OTTER
Otter hunting was once considered a sport, and it still occurs in some parts of the world, although in many countries otters are now protected by law. Today, these creatures face new threats: the development of waterways for angling and leisure pursuits, and the pollution of streams, rivers, and lakes.

PLAY TIME
Otters spend much time at play, either on their own or with one another. Such games may help to improve their hunting skills.

Beaver skull

NATURE'S LOGGERS
Beavers cut down trees for food and also to build homes in lakes they create for themselves (below left). They eat waterweeds, leaves, and other plant matter.

Large incisor teeth for gnawing

Molar teeth for grinding food

GNAWING TEETH
The beaver's large, chisel-like front teeth (typical of rodents) can gnaw through tree trunks with ease.

FLAT SLAP
The beaver's tail is flattened and scaly. Besides its use as a rudder and paddle, it can be slapped on the water's surface to warn other beavers of danger.

Beaver

Beaver tail

Frogs, toads, and newts

AMPHIBIANS ARE ANIMALS that never quite set themselves free of the water. As their name suggests (*amphi* for "both", and *bios* for "life"), they lead a double life: in the water when young, and out of it when adult. Many adult amphibians on land must stay in damp places so that they do not dry out. This is because some species take in oxygen through the skin, as well as breathing it into their lungs, and only moist skin will absorb oxygen. Young amphibians just hatched from their eggs also absorb dissolved oxygen from the water through their skin, in addition to having gills for breathing. Some amphibians, like the common frog and toad, prefer still water in which to breed. Others, such as the hellbender, a huge salamander from North America, frequent fast-flowing water. This may be because there is more dissolved oxygen in moving water than in still water, and such large amphibians need an abundant supply. Amphibians are divided into two main groups, distinguished by their tails: newts and salamanders have them, while frogs and toads do not (except as tadpoles).

CLUMPED TOGETHER
Common frogs lay eggs (spawn) in clumps that float below the surface. Spawn from several females may collect in one large mass.

Developing tadpole

Common frog spawn

STRUNG OUT
The common toad's spawn forms a black-speckled jelly necklace about 2 m (6 ft) long. It is often seen wrapped around plant stems.

PATCHY PATTERNING
Common frogs vary in colour, but in general they are mottled with patches of olive-green and brown.

Developing tadpole

Common toad spawn

Tiger salamander

WARNING COLOURATION
The tiger salamander's patterning of black with bright-yellow blotches is believed to be a warning signal. The vivid colouring tells predators that the salamander's skin and glands produce foul-tasting secretions.

Warning colouration

One-year-old common frog

Tympanum

Golden-lined frog

GOLDEN EARS
Like other frogs, the golden-lined frog has good hearing – vital for finding mates by the sound of their breeding calls. The frog's ear (tympanum) is the disc-shaped membrane behind its eye.

Unwebbed fore feet

Common toad

Cuban tree frog

Rounded fingertips with sticky pads

STICKY FINGERS
This Cuban tree frog has rounded, sticky pads on its digits, which help it to grip leaves and twigs. Adults spend all their time in trees, leaving them only to lay their eggs in a pond.

DRESSED IN GREEN
The startlingly green skin of Australia's dwarf tree frog gives good concealment among the bright leaves of its forest home.

Dwarf tree frog

GOING FOR A WALK
The squat, heavily built common toad prefers to move by walking in an unhurried fashion, though it can leap a short way when at risk. The toad's toes are webbed, but its fingers are not.

Mottled skin for camouflage

Webbed hind feet

GREEN TOAD
The green toad (left) is smaller and slimmer than the common toad, and can run surprisingly fast. It is often confused with the natterjack toad (below).

Green toad

TIME TO GO
Natterjack toads tend to spawn in shallow, temporary pools. In summer, crowds of toadlets prepare to leave the water.

Natterjack toadlets

Natterjack spawn

Developing tadpole

NATTERJACK SPAWN
The natterjack toad lays a single row of eggs among pebbles or plant stems.

A BIG EATER
All adult frogs and toads are carnivores. Big frogs have big mouths that can swallow large food items. There are several reliable reports of American bullfrogs eating bats!

American bullfrog

SUBMARINE HUNTER
The palmate newt spends part of the year on land, hibernating or feeding at night on worms and other small animals. It returns to the pond in spring to court and lay eggs.

Mandarin newt

Developing newtlet

Newt eggs

Palmate newt

Warning colouration

FABLED FROGS
The fable-writer Aesop told of the hare's dissatisfaction at being prey to so many animals. But when it saw the frog's plight, it felt less hard done by.

RED FOR DANGER!
Like the tiger salamander opposite, the mandarin newt of Asia has bright colours warning that it makes a foul mouthful.

SINGLE EGGS
Most newt species lay their eggs singly, attaching them to leaves and waterweeds. Some species wrap each egg carefully in a leaf for protection.

MATING
Early spring is a time of commotion in the pond, as amphibians gather to breed. The male common frog struggles with rivals to find a female, and then takes up a piggyback position. He may stay there for many days, clasping her slippery chest skin tightly with roughened pads on his thumbs. As the eggs are laid, he sheds sperm over them. The exhausted pair then part company.

A FOAM NEST
The foam-nest tree frog whips up a bubbly nest, to keep the spawn moist. When grown, tadpoles drop out into the pond beneath.

MALE MIDWIFE
The midwife toad gathers the egg string and carries it around his back legs for up to a month. As the tadpoles begin to hatch, he releases them into a pool.

18th-century engraving of a male midwife toad carrying its eggs

Hunters in the water

MORE THAN 300 MILLION YEARS AGO, the reptiles appeared on Earth. They probably evolved from amphibians (pp.38–39). Their big advantage was that they had made a complete break from an aquatic environment. Unlike amphibians, which needed water in which to lay their jelly-covered eggs, reptiles had hard-shelled eggs that could be laid on land. Soon, as dinosaurs, they would come to dominate life on land. Since that time, however, some groups of reptiles have made an evolutionary U-turn and gone back to life in the water. Many snakes readily take to water, swim well, and hunt fish, frogs, aquatic insects, and land creatures that come to the pond or riverside for a drink. Indeed, certain groups of reptiles, such as crocodiles and turtles, have never really left the aquatic environment, though they come on to land to lay their eggs.

Anaconda

GIANT IN THE WATER
The anaconda, or water boa, of northern South America is the world's heaviest snake, and also one of the longest. Specimens measuring as much as 9 m (30 ft) long and weighing in excess of 200 kg (440 lb) have been recorded. This giant snake lives in swamps, marshes, and slow-moving streams in tropical rain forests. It preys on a variety of fish, birds, reptiles, and mammals. Its jaws dislocate and open so wide that it can consume creatures as large as pigs.

Water moccasin

DOWN IN THE SWAMPS
This old engraving shows the water moccasin, a venomous swamp-dweller of the southeastern USA. When this snake feels threatened, it opens its mouth wide to reveal the white lining inside, hence its other name – the cottonmouth. The water moccasin may also try to deter would-be attackers by releasing an unpleasant-smelling secretion from glands near the base of its tail.

Body is covered in thick, waterproof scales

Viperine water snake

Zig-zag markings on the snake's back are similar to those of a common viper, or adder

Snake swims by undulating its body

Long, streamlined shape enables snake to move easily through the water

Turtle … or terrapin?

There is little biological distinction between a turtle and a terrapin. Most experts call the entire group (chelonians) turtles. Small, freshwater species may be named terrapins, from a Native American word that referred originally to the diamondback terrapin. But the numerous exceptions confuse the issue. Whatever our labels, however, many turtles are well equipped for an aquatic life, either in fresh water or in the sea. Some have webbed or flipper-like feet, and leathery skin overlying the shell on their underside, through which oxygen can be absorbed. They tend to be omnivores, taking aquatic creatures, fruits from bankside trees, and carrion (dead animals) whenever they become available.

SCARCELY A RIPPLE
The viperine water snake of Europe is quite at home in the water, swimming easily across its surface. It will strike at virtually any suitably sized prey, from fish to frogs and even small mammals. Adults grow to 80 cm (2.5 ft) or more (this one is approximately life-sized, but young). Despite its name and its zig-zag markings reminiscent of the adder, it is not poisonous, being a relative of the grass snake.

Yellow-bellied terrapin

Distinctive brown and yellow markings

OPPOSITE FEET FORWARDS
The yellow-bellied terrapin may walk along the bed of a river or lake, or swim by paddling alternately with two limbs – the front foot on one side and the back foot on the other.

Left foreleg is forward when right foreleg is back

Smooth plates on shell

Ridged bony plates on shell

Common snapper

Long, fleshy tail has a crest like an alligator's

Soft-shelled turtle

Snorkel-like nostrils

Strong horny jaws in mouth

Shell lacks bony plates

Webbed feet for swimming

THE SOFT SHELL
Soft-shelled turtles have leathery shells that lack the rigid, bony plates carried by their hard-shelled relatives. Their snorkel-like nostrils allow them to take in air from the surface while their bodies are submerged. This life-sized youngster will grow to about 30 cm (1 ft) long.

SNAPPY CUSTOMER
This young common snapper will reach almost 50 cm (20 in) when adult. Its sharp-ridged jaws will be strong enough to crack the shells of other turtles, which will form part of its diet.

WIDE-RANGING TASTES
Water snakes are not fussy eaters, and most species will eat all kinds of freshwater life – including this unfortunate frog!

Nostrils are on top of the lizard's snout, which helps it to breathe when swimming

Spiny crest formed from enlarged scales

Eastern water dragon

DIVING DRAGON
Eastern water dragons frequent watercourses in eastern Australia. This lizard swims powerfully, using its vertically flattened tail and long legs. It has a body length of nearly 30 cm (1 ft), and a tail that is more than three times as long, at 1 m (3 ft). The eastern water dragon has a varied diet, ranging from worms and frogs to shellfish, small mammals, and fruits.

Floating flowers

IN ANCIENT TIMES, people were amazed to see that, when a previously dry watercourse filled with recent rains, the splendid blooms of water-lilies would soon appear. These aquatic plants gained a reputation as a symbol of immortality; the ancient Egyptians even worshipped one type of water-lily, the sacred lotus. Water-lily flowers are made more mysterious by their daily routine: they remain closed during the morning, open to reveal their beauty at around noon, and towards evening close again and sometimes sink slightly into the water. This may be an adaptation to aid pollination by flying insects, which are more likely to be active in the afternoon's warmth. On overcast days the flowers might not open fully at all. This is because dull weather signifies wind and rain, so the closed flowers are less likely to be swamped. The leaves and flowers grow on tough, rubbery stems – 3 m (10 ft) long in some species – anchored in the mud on the beds of ponds, lakes, and slow rivers.

Flowerbud

BEAUTIFUL NUISANCE
The water hyacinth is an attractive, free-floating flowering plant. Despite its beauty, many people consider it a nuisance plant because it spreads so rapidly that it often cloggs rivers, canals, and ditches.

Attractive flower makes the water hyacinth a popular choice for ornamental ponds

Water hyacinth

Leaves may be heart-shaped, oval, or round

Red hybrid – "Escarboucle"

Yellow water-lily leaves are patterned with a red tinge

White water-lily flower

Leathery leaf repels water droplets

Pink hybrid

Conspicuous yellow stamens

LILIES AND THEIR HYBRIDS
There are some 60 species of water-lily around
the world (in some areas they are known as
lotuses). Their beautiful, waxy-looking flowers and
bold, circular leaves have made them favourites in
ponds, ornamental water gardens, and landscaped
lakes. Horticulturalists have bred many differently
coloured flowers.

Yellow hybrid –
"Chromatella"

Waxy petals

Pink hybrid

FLOATING SAUCERS
Some of the largest leaves of any plant belong
to the Amazonian water-lily. A single leaf may
be more than 1.5 m (5 ft) across, with an
upturned rim and stiff reinforcing ribs beneath.

LILY-LEAF CASE
The caterpillar of the china mark moth cuts out
an oval of leaf from a lily pad. It glues the oval
to the underside of the pad with silk thread, to
form a protective
case in which
it can
hide.

Water-lily
leaf

WELL-USED LEAVES
Water-lily leaves, or pads as they are often known, are used by
many aquatic creatures. Pond snails browse on them and lay their
speckled, jelly-sausage egg masses (p.8) on their undersides. Frogs
rest on or under them, waiting to snap up unwary insects. In some
places, the pads grow so densely that certain creatures can even
walk on them. The jacana bird of Africa has long, widespread toes
and is known as the lily trotter, since it can often be seen stepping
delicately on the leaves in its search for insects and seeds.

Plants at the pond's surface

MANY WATER PLANTS are not rooted in the mud at the bottom of the pond, but are free to float over the surface of the water. Most have trailing roots that balance the plant and absorb minerals, although some have no roots at all. At first sight, these plants seem to have few problems. Unlike some land plants, they are well supported and, out in the middle of the pond, they cannot be shaded by trees or taller plants. But there are disadvantages – the water's surface can be whipped by the wind into waves that drag and tear at them, rain might collect on a leaf and sink it, or the leaf may be frozen under water.

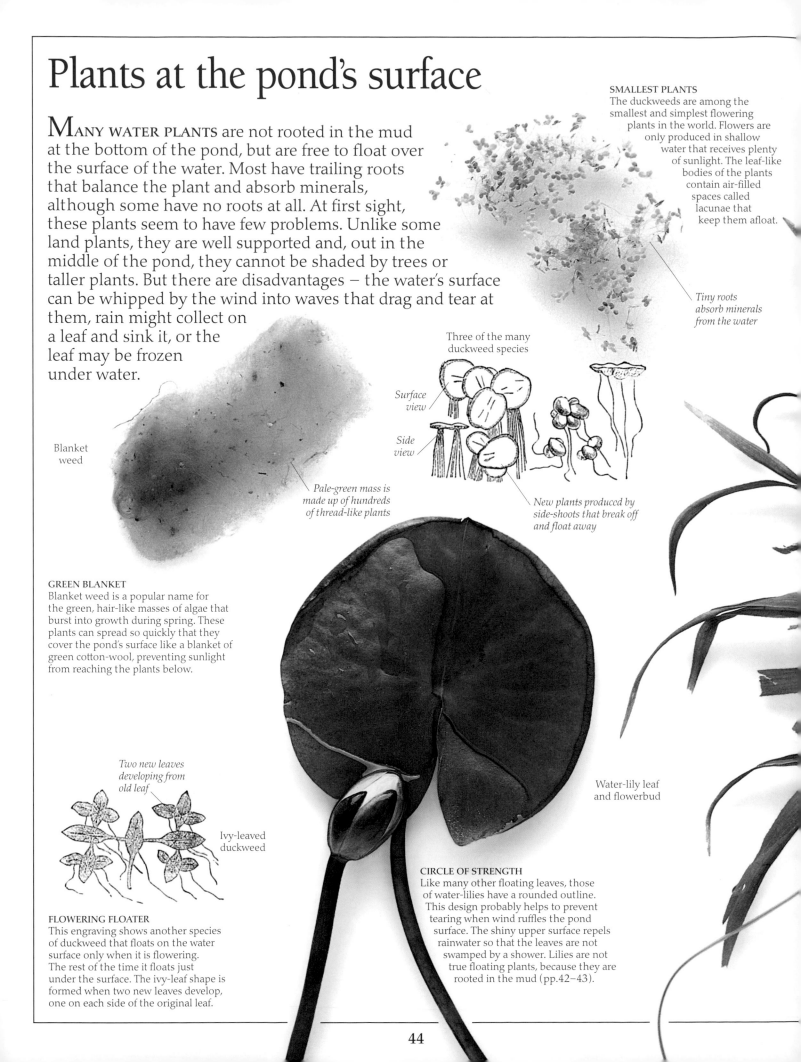

SMALLEST PLANTS
The duckweeds are among the smallest and simplest flowering plants in the world. Flowers are only produced in shallow water that receives plenty of sunlight. The leaf-like bodies of the plants contain air-filled spaces called lacunae that keep them afloat.

Tiny roots absorb minerals from the water

Blanket weed

Pale-green mass is made up of hundreds of thread-like plants

Three of the many duckweed species

Surface view

Side view

New plants produced by side-shoots that break off and float away

GREEN BLANKET
Blanket weed is a popular name for the green, hair-like masses of algae that burst into growth during spring. These plants can spread so quickly that they cover the pond's surface like a blanket of green cotton-wool, preventing sunlight from reaching the plants below.

Two new leaves developing from old leaf

Ivy-leaved duckweed

Water-lily leaf and flowerbud

FLOWERING FLOATER
This engraving shows another species of duckweed that floats on the water surface only when it is flowering. The rest of the time it floats just under the surface. The ivy-leaf shape is formed when two new leaves develop, one on each side of the original leaf.

CIRCLE OF STRENGTH
Like many other floating leaves, those of water-lilies have a rounded outline. This design probably helps to prevent tearing when wind ruffles the pond surface. The shiny upper surface repels rainwater so that the leaves are not swamped by a shower. Lilies are not true floating plants, because they are rooted in the mud (pp.42–43).

Azolla water fern

Pink tinge turns to deep red in autumn

Thread-like roots trail beneath the plant

WINTER SEEDS AND BUDS
Frogbit, a relative of water soldier (below), has a similar technique for avoiding the ice and frost of winter. In this case, however, the parts that overwinter are the seeds and the dense, specially grown winter buds. Both are produced in the autumn and sink to rest in the mud, until the increasing light levels and temperatures of spring spur them into growth, when they float to the surface again. In summer, the delicate white flowers and kidney-shaped leaves carpet whole ponds and ditches.

Leaves are similar in shape to water-lily leaves

FLOATING FRONDS
Azolla is not a flowering plant but a fern, so technically its delicately sculptured leaves are called fronds. Tiny hairs repel water and prevent the fronds from becoming waterlogged and sinking.

Frogbit

Plants will sometimes root in shallow water

Water soldier

Trailing roots

GREEN ROSETTES
The rosettes of water soldier spend summer floating at or near the pond surface. As autumn approaches, the leaves develop a slimy coating that weighs them down. The plant sinks, to avoid winter's frost and ice. Fresh spring leaves buoy it up again. This plant reproduces by sending out runners that root at a distance, and by male and female flowers borne on separate plants.

SOLDIER IN FLOWER
Water soldier produces white flowers in midsummer, with male and female flowers forming on different plants. Once the flowering period is over, the plant sinks to the bottom of the pond.

Long, unbranched roots hang down under the plant to balance it

Underwater weeds

Submerged weeds grow in ponds and rivers like trees in a miniature underwater forest. They provide shelter for some animals, and places of ambush for others, enabling them to dash out and grab unwary victims swimming by. Weeds are food for many creatures, from pond snails to ducks. They also provide that most vital substance, oxygen. As a plant carries out photosynthesis, capturing the Sun's light energy to build new tissues, it produces oxygen as a by-product. The oxygen diffuses into the water and is used by both plants and animals for the process of respiration. On a sunny day, small bubbles of oxygen can be seen coating underwater plants and occasionally rising to the surface.

Rigid hornwort

CURTAIN OF ROOTS
The water violet's abundant roots hang like a veil in the water. The stem grows out of the water, where it bears not leaves but pale, pinkish, five-petalled flowers.

TOTAL SUBMERSION
Feathery-looking hornworts are completely at home in the water. Even the flowers are submerged, growing at the junction of the leaf and the stem.

Water violet

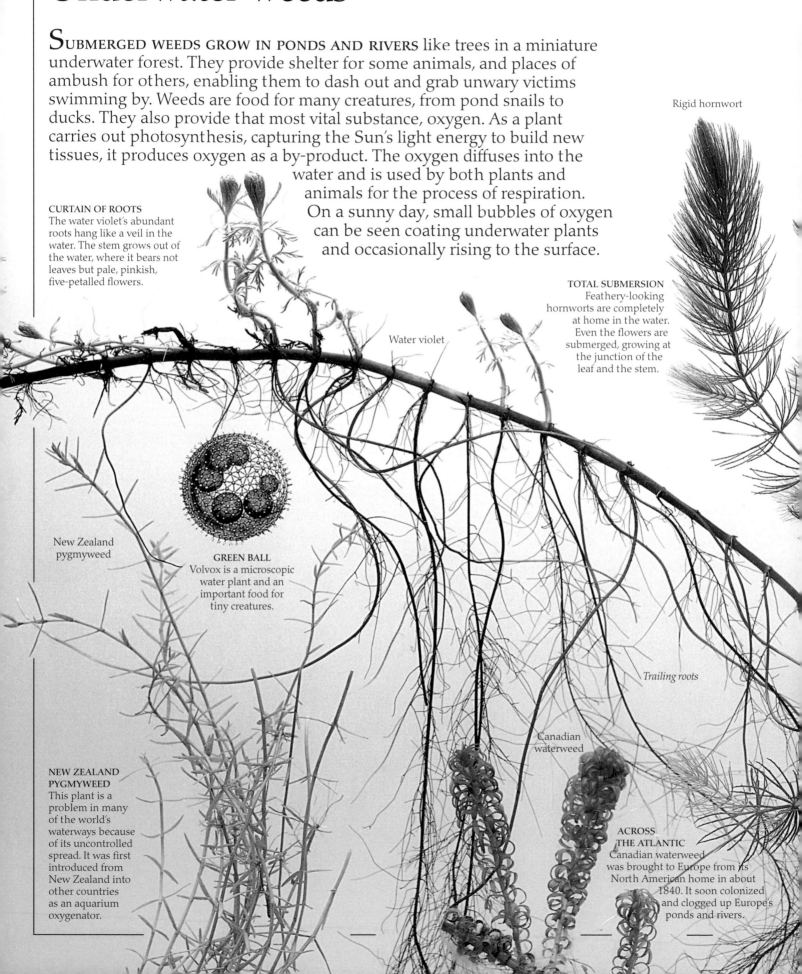

New Zealand pygmyweed

GREEN BALL
Volvox is a microscopic water plant and an important food for tiny creatures.

Trailing roots

Canadian waterweed

NEW ZEALAND PYGMYWEED
This plant is a problem in many of the world's waterways because of its uncontrolled spread. It was first introduced from New Zealand into other countries as an aquarium oxygenator.

ACROSS THE ATLANTIC
Canadian waterweed was brought to Europe from its North American home in about 1840. It soon colonized and clogged up Europe's ponds and rivers.

POND PLANKTON
At 25x magnification, the microscopic world of underwater plants is revealed.

Narrow leaf resembles fir tree needle

Bulbous rush

PERCH IN THE GRASS
Tape grass offers a hidcout for many fish, including the perch, which is camouflaged among the plant's leaves by the vertical stripes on its body (p.23).

Tape grass

SLENDER WATERWEED
The pale-green water starwort sways in clumps in the water.

FLUSHED RUSH
The bulbous rush is usually rooted on the pondside, but sometimes it grows under water, becoming very elongated.

Water starwort

Dragonflies and damselflies

Broad-bodied libellula nymph

Young southern hawker nymph

Mask — Hooks on mask impale prey — *Mask*

WITH SOME SPECIES able to fly at speeds of 50 kph (30 mph) or more, dragonflies are fierce airborne predators. They race to and fro along the bank and over the water's surface, seeking out flying prey such as midges and gnats with their huge eyes. Like those of other insects, dragonfly eyes are made up of many separate lenses that probably give a mosaic-like picture of the world. As the adults dart about above the water, the aquatic nymphs crawl on the pond bottom. They eat any small creature they can seize, from other water insects to tadpoles and fish.

THE DEADLY MASK
Dragonfly nymphs are the scourge of the pond, eating anything they can catch with their mask. This is a horny flap, equivalent to the lower lip, which has two vicious hooks at the end (above). Normally the mask is folded under the head, but it is hinged so that it can suddenly shoot out to impale prey, which is then pulled back into the mouth.

Damselflies

These are smaller and more slender relatives of dragonflies. Although at first glance they appear very similar in shape and lifestyle, there are several important differences that distinguish them from the dragonflies. The most obvious is that a damselfly holds its two pairs of wings together over its back when resting, while a dragonfly holds them out flat at the sides of its body.

Discarded skin

CAST-OFF CLOTHING
This perfectly detailed empty skin is from a brown hawker dragonfly's final moult. New adults usually emerge at night or early in the morning, to avoid predators.

THE MATING GAME
During mating, the male dragonfly clasps the female, and she bends to pick up the sperm from a special organ at the front of his abdomen.

SIMILAR WINGS
A damselfly's wings are roughly equal in size, with rounded ends, unlike the dragonfly's wings.

Blue-tailed damselfly

Emerald damselfly

Eyes protrude from side of head

Rounded wing tips

MALE AND FEMALE
In most damselflies, the female has a slightly wider and less colourful abdomen than the male.

Azure damselfly

Large red damselfly

SMALLER EYES
The small eyes of the damselfly are set on the sides of the head, while dragonflies' eyes meet at the top of the head.

WEAK FLIERS
Damselflies tend to be weaker fliers than their dragonfly cousins.

THE LIFE OF THE DRAGONFLY
A dragonfly begins life as an egg laid in water. It hatches into a larva that grows by splitting its skin and forming a new, larger skin. There are 8–15 moults over two years or more, depending on the species. A gradual change like this from larva to adult – compared with a sudden change, such as from caterpillar to butterfly – is called incomplete metamorphosis. The intermediate larval stages are referred to as nymphs. Finally, the nymph climbs up a stem into the air, splits its skin for one last time, and the adult dragonfly emerges.

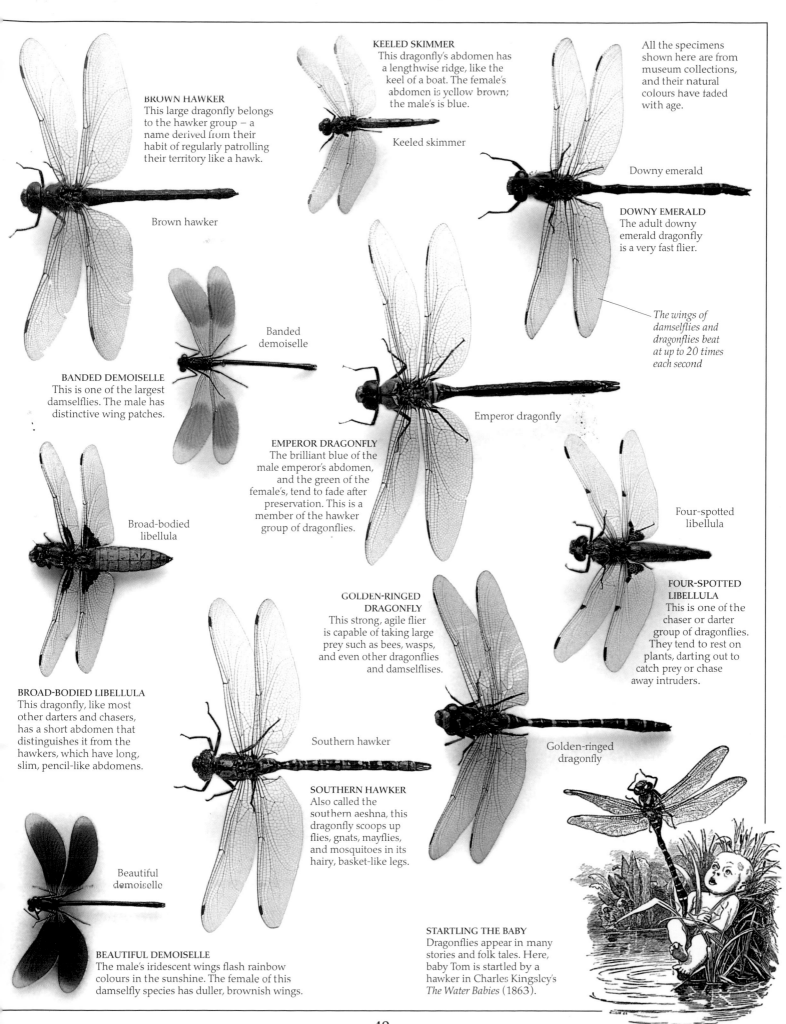

BROWN HAWKER
This large dragonfly belongs to the hawker group – a name derived from their habit of regularly patrolling their territory like a hawk.

Brown hawker

KEELED SKIMMER
This dragonfly's abdomen has a lengthwise ridge, like the keel of a boat. The female's abdomen is yellow brown; the male's is blue.

Keeled skimmer

All the specimens shown here are from museum collections, and their natural colours have faded with age.

Downy emerald

DOWNY EMERALD
The adult downy emerald dragonfly is a very fast flier.

The wings of damselflies and dragonflies beat at up to 20 times each second

Banded demoiselle

BANDED DEMOISELLE
This is one of the largest damselflies. The male has distinctive wing patches.

Broad-bodied libellula

EMPEROR DRAGONFLY
The brilliant blue of the male emperor's abdomen, and the green of the female's, tend to fade after preservation. This is a member of the hawker group of dragonflies.

Emperor dragonfly

Four-spotted libellula

FOUR-SPOTTED LIBELLULA
This is one of the chaser or darter group of dragonflies. They tend to rest on plants, darting out to catch prey or chase away intruders.

BROAD-BODIED LIBELLULA
This dragonfly, like most other darters and chasers, has a short abdomen that distinguishes it from the hawkers, which have long, slim, pencil-like abdomens.

GOLDEN-RINGED DRAGONFLY
This strong, agile flier is capable of taking large prey such as bees, wasps, and even other dragonflies and damselflies.

Southern hawker

Golden-ringed dragonfly

SOUTHERN HAWKER
Also called the southern aeshna, this dragonfly scoops up flies, gnats, mayflies, and mosquitoes in its hairy, basket-like legs.

Beautiful demoiselle

BEAUTIFUL DEMOISELLE
The male's iridescent wings flash rainbow colours in the sunshine. The female of this damselfly species has duller, brownish wings.

STARTLING THE BABY
Dragonflies appear in many stories and folk tales. Here, baby Tom is startled by a hawker in Charles Kingsley's *The Water Babies* (1863).

49

Insects in the water

Gerris water strider

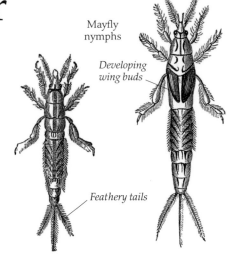

Mayfly nymphs

Developing wing buds

Feathery tails

THE MOST ADAPTABLE CREATURES on Earth, insects can live in places ranging from glaciers to hot springs, and deserts to tropical forests. About half of the 25 major groups of insects live in fresh water. Some, such as water beetles and bugs, spend nearly all their lives in water. Others, like mayflies and caddis flies, have a watery "childhood" and emerge into the air when adult. Certain aquatic insects, including the water beetles, are air-breathing and visit the surface regularly to obtain supplies, which they store by various ingenious means. Others have specialized gills to extract oxygen from the water, and there are even insects that can absorb dissolved oxygen through their skin.

BUDDING MAYFLIES
Like dragonfly larvae (p.48), mayfly larvae are called nymphs. As the nymph matures, small wing buds grow with each moult.

Rat-tailed maggots (drone fly larvae)

Adult drone fly

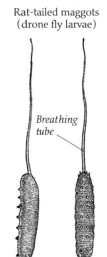

Breathing tube

MAGGOT'S PARENT
The rat-tailed maggot (left) is the larva of the drone fly, a type of hoverfly named for its resemblance to the drones of the honey bee.

Adult mayfly

Long tails identify this insect

THREE-TAILED FLY
Like its larvae (top right), the adult mayfly has three very distinctive trailing tails. Mayflies are known as spinners by anglers.

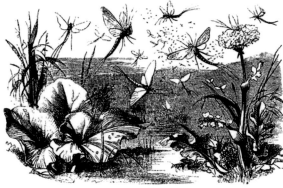

SPRING FEAST
Mayfly adults emerge in huge swarms in spring. They fly weakly, have no mouths and so cannot feed, and spend their few days of adult life mating and laying eggs by dipping their abdomens in water. Their dance-like flight, known as the "dance of the mayflies", attracts hungry fish – and anglers, who use mayfly lures to catch trout.

MAGGOT WITH SNORKEL
The rat-tailed maggot has a long breathing tube made up of three sections that telescope into one another. It lives in the mud of shallow ponds, sucking up decaying food.

STICKS AND STONES
Many species of caddis fly have aquatic larvae that build protective cases around themselves. Each species uses different materials to build its case. As the larva grows, it adds more material to the front of the case.

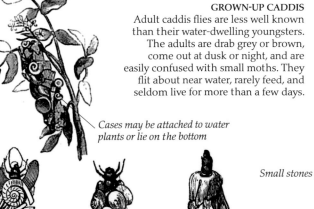

Cases may be attached to water plants or lie on the bottom

GROWN-UP CADDIS
Adult caddis flies are less well known than their water-dwelling youngsters. The adults are drab grey or brown, come out at dusk or night, and are easily confused with small moths. They flit about near water, rarely feed, and seldom live for more than a few days.

Adult caddis flies

Wings covered with fine hairs

Antennae are often as long as the body

Plant stalks

Small stones

Discarded snail shells

Entrance to case

Case is extended by adding extra material

Larva pokes its head out to feed

Each species makes a distinctive case

Engravings of caddis-fly larval cases

Actual cases built by caddis-fly larvae

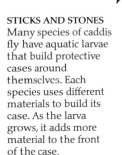

50

Front legs seize prey

Water stick insect

Front legs catch tadpoles and other prey

Water scorpion

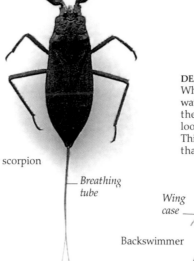

Water scorpion

Water scorpion

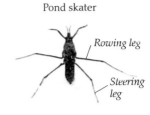

Pond skater

Rowing leg

Steering leg

SPINDLY STALKER
The water stick insect grabs any small underwater creature with its mantis-like front legs, and then sucks the juices from inside the victim's body using its needle-like mouthparts. A short trip to the surface allows fresh supplies of air to be collected through the long tail, the two parts of which are usually held together by bristles to form a tube.

Parts of breathing tube

Breathing tube

STING IN THE TAIL?
Unlike its land-dwelling namesake, the water scorpion does not have a poisonous sting in its "tail", which is actually a harmless breathing tube. The dangerous parts are its powerful, claw-like front legs and beak-shaped mouth.

DEAD LEAF?
When disturbed, the water scorpion sinks to the bottom and stays still, looking like a dead leaf. This is a smaller species than the one on the left.

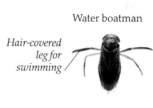

Wing case

Backswimmer

BACKSWIMMER
Beetle-like in appearance, the backswimmer is really a bug. This view from above shows the hard cases that cover its strong flying wings. The backswimmer spends most of its time upside-down, hanging from the surface.

WATER-WALKER
The back four feet of the bug known as the pond skater have thick pads of hair that repel water. They prevent the bug from sinking as it rows across the pond's surface.

Water boatman

Hair-covered leg for swimming

WATER BOATMAN
This insect's name refers to the oar-like rowing motions of its legs as it propels itself through the water. It eats any plant debris or algae it can catch with its sieve-like front legs.

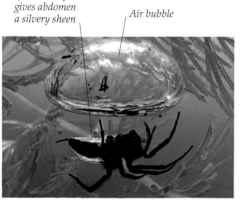

Air trapped on spider's body gives abdomen a silvery sheen

Air bubble

THE BUBBLE CHAMBER
The air-breathing water spider (not actually an insect, but an arachnid), makes a "diving bell" to live in. It weaves a web among water plants and stocks it with air (below). The spider collects air at the surface, trapping it among its body hairs. As the spider swims back down to its home, the trapped air gives its abdomen a silvery sheen.

BEETLE POWER
In a small pond, the great diving beetle has few predators, but many prey. Its victims include insects, tadpoles, and small fish such as this unlucky stickleback.

Water spiders and their "diving bell" homes

SPARE AIR
Water beetles are air-breathing aquatic insects that have devised clever methods for collecting air from the surface. Some beetles trap air on the hairs under their bodies, while others capture it under their wing cases. The silver water beetle, shown here, uses both methods. The air they carry makes them buoyant, but it also means that they have to struggle hard to swim downwards.

Silver water beetle

Freshwater shells

ALL THE LIFE-SIZED shells shown here have two features in common: their builder-owners live in fresh water, and they belong to the mollusc group. A mollusc's shell is made chiefly of calcium-containing minerals such as calcium carbonate (lime). To make its shell, the animal must absorb minerals from the water. In general, aquatic molluscs are more common in hard-water areas, where water is naturally rich in dissolved minerals, than in soft-water areas, where the water has a lower mineral content. The snails and limpets (gastropods) are mostly grazers, feeding on water plants and the algae that grow on submerged stones, although some species can filter-feed. The mussels and cockles (bivalves) feed by sucking in a stream of water and filtering out tiny food particles.

SWAN MUSSEL
The growth rings on this swan mussel's shell show that it is about six or seven years old.

How molluscs breathe

Water snails are divided into two groups, depending on how they breathe. Like land snails, the great pond snail, ramshorn snail, and bladder snail breathe air, and are known as the pulmonates. They float up to the surface, open a breathing aperture, and take a gulp of air into a lung-like cavity. The other group, including valve snails, river snails, and spire snails, is called the prosobranchs. They breathe by absorbing oxygen from the water through gills.

RIGHT-HANDERS
Most great pond snail shells curl to the right, but "left-handers" also occur.

DUCK MUSSEL
This bivalve's shell is more swollen than that of the swan mussel.

SEE-THROUGH SNAIL
The nautilus ramshorn is so small that its shell is semi-transparent.

FAVOURITE FOOD
Pea mussels are the staple food of many fish and waterbirds.

WANDERING SNAIL
The whorls of the wandering snail's shell are compressed at the tip.

CURLY WHORLY
The tightly coiled white ramshorn is found in ponds and streams.

MARBLED SNAIL
The nerite snail has an attractively stippled and whorled shell.

JOINTED SHELL
The horny pea cockle is a bivalve, meaning that it has two hinged parts to its shell, called valves.

River shellfish

The molluscs below and left (swan and duck mussels) tend to frequent flowing water, compared to the still waters of ponds and lakes. The growth rings of the mussels indicate their age, which might be up to a dozen years for a large individual. Growth rings can be seen on snails, too, but they are less clearly divided into a year-by-year pattern.

NEW GROWTH
As a snail grows, it adds new material at the open end of the shell to enlarge its home

TWISTING TUBE
Snail shells are coiled, gradually widening tubes, clearly seen on this Lister's river snail.

MINERAL COLLECTOR
River snails' shells may be more than 5 cm (2 in) long – that's a lot of calcium to collect!

LISTENING SNAIL
The ear pond snail's flared opening resembles a human ear.

Umbo is the oldest part of the shell

SWOLLEN JOINT
Called the swollen river mussel, this bivalve has a projection known as an umbo near its hinge joint.

ZEBRA MUSSEL
This bivalve anchors itself to rocks by strong, sticky fibres known as byssus threads.

WATERWEED EATER
The great ramshorn water snail browses on underwater plants.

DISTINCTIVE SHELL
The last whorl on the bladder snail's shell is large compared to the other whorls.

STUBBY AND SHINY
These shiny, compact shells belong to the common bithynia.

LEACH'S BITHYNIA
This snail is host to an intermediate form of the cat liver fluke parasite.

STRAIGHT SNAIL
The river limpet is a true snail, but its shell is not coiled.

OPEN AND SHUT
The valve of the valve snail is the door, or operculum, of its shell.

SLOW WATER
The lake limpet can often be found in slow-flowing rivers.

OPENING THE DOOR
The operculum, or door, to the shell allows the snail to emerge to feed.

Operculum makes a watertight seal to the shell when it closes

FILTER-FEEDERS
Pea cockles are tiny, filter-feeding bivalve molluscs.

SALTY AND FRESH
Jenkin's spire shells are found in estuaries, and also in ponds and rivers.

Head of the river

Many rivers begin life as fast-flowing upland streams, cascading across moors or through craggy woodlands. The deep, rocky gulleys, the overhanging trees, and the splashing waters create contrasting worlds – shady, damp banks with lush vegetation, and stream beds where rushing water washes away the majority of plant life and all but the most tenaciously clinging animals. In a flood, entire plant and animal communities may be swept away. Yet new seeds and spores soon spring up, while creatures creep out from under rocks to fight their way back upstream.

Dipper

UNDERWATER WALKER
The dipper bobs its head as it stands on midstream rocks, watching for small animal prey. It can also walk along the bed of the river, with its head facing upstream and using the pressure of the current on its wings and tail to keep its feet firmly on the bottom.

ARMOURED CRAYFISH
Hard water (p.52) is favoured by the freshwater crayfish, a relative of the marine lobster. It needs plenty of calcium minerals to build its shell.

Hard outer shell made up from minerals in the water

Freshwater crayfish

BANKSIDE MOISTURE-LOVERS
Succulent growths of mosses, liverworts, ferns, and other damp-loving plants colonize the banks and splash-zone rocks.

Polytrichum moss

Puffball

Fern

Bankside plants

Liverwort

YOUNG BALL
Fungi, such as this young member of the puffball group, relish shady streamside conditions.

LICHEN BRANCH
Shady, damp conditions are ideal for certain lichens, which are cooperative combinations of fungi and algae. Two different kinds of leafy lichen are growing on this branch.

Marsh violet

Great woodrush

Liverwort

Bullhead

UPSTREAM FISH
Despite the fast current, some fish, including the bullhead, have adapted to life at the head of the river. The bullhead's flattened shape allows it to hide under stones on the riverbed.

Oak leaves

FOOD FROM ABOVE
Trees such as the oak hang over the water, and their fruits and leaves provide sustenance for river-dwellers if they fall into the water.

Fontinalis moss

Acorns

Galls caused by insects living in oak leaves

Deeply divided fronds

Great woodrush

UNDERWATER MOSS
Fontinalis, or willow moss, undulates with the current in slower streams and rivers, anchored to a stone or fallen log.

BETWEEN THE BOULDERS
Groups of midstream boulders often support a thriving island of life. Here, great woodrush sprouts from current-collected soil.

Shiny, undivided frond

Rows of spores

Male fern

Layer of moss growing on boulders

FEATHERY FRONDS
Many types of fern thrive in the shaded, humid conditions along riverbanks. The hart's-tongue fern (far right) has rib-like rows of brown spore cases on the undersides of its fronds. It is unusual among ferns in having solid, unbranched fronds.

Feathery, pale-green fronds

Shiny, dark-green fronds

Hard fern

Lady fern

Hart's-tongue fern

Brown spore cases

Life along the riverbank

As STREAMS BECOME MORE SEDATE, and their courses join up and widen, the river comes into being. But when does a stream become a river? One definition is that streams are less than 5 m (15 ft) wide, while rivers are wider. Larger rivers usually have a slower current, allowing rooted plants to flourish at the water's edge. Whatever the distinction, riverbank life suits many kinds of plants and animals. On a high-banked river, the soil at the water's edge is nearly always saturated, but it becomes drier higher up the bank. So there is often a characteristic zonation of plant life, with mud-rooted irises and water plantains lower down, and the damp-ground hemp agrimony, balsam, and similar flowers slightly higher up.

Great burdock

Thistle-shaped flowerhead

Messing about on the river has long been a favourite leisure pursuit

FIVE IN ONE
Each small flower of hemp agrimony is actually a cluster of five even smaller florets.

ABOUT TO FLOWER
This teasel's flower is just emerging, but its pinkish-mauve petals are not yet visible.

Teasel

Spiny flowerhead is still developing

Hooks attach fruit to passing animals

Heart-shaped leaf is slightly downy

Explosive seed cases develop inside the flower

Leaf has toothed edges

Hemp agrimony

HITCHING A RIDE
Young great burdock flowers (right) bear the hooks that, when the seeds ripen, will catch on fur and clothes.

TRAVELLING FLOWER
Indian, or Himalayan, balsam, a native of that region, was cultivated in other countries for its flowers. It has now spread along riverbanks, ditch sides, and damp gulleys in many parts of the world.

Leaf has serrated margins

Stem has reddish tinge

Indian balsam (Himalayan balsam)

HIGH-WATER MARK
The river's spring flood left surface debris stuck to this overhanging twig, 1 m (3 ft) above summer's water level.

Old plant stalks wrapped around a twig

PICTURESQUE PLANTAIN
The plant's tall, pyramidal inflorescences make water plantain a dramatic sight on the riverbank.

Water plantain leaf

Water plantain inflorescence

AFTERNOON OPENING
Water plantain roots in the mud at the edges of small rivers. Its flowers are closed for most of the morning and evening, and open only after noon.

Tiny lilac flower

Toothmarks of mammal

Yellow flag leaves

ANONYMOUS NIBBLER
These yellow flag leaves from a steep riverbank have been nibbled by a foraging mammal.

RIVERBANK HOME
Many mammals use the riverbank as a home. Otters make well-hidden dens called holts among the bank vegetation or under overhanging tree roots.

Flatworm

Freshwater shrimp

DOWN IN THE MUD
The beds of ponds and rivers abound with small creatures such as these, which are food for fish and other animals.

Caddis-fly larva has built its case from tiny pebbles (p.50)

Flatworm

Freshwater shrimp

Loaches

BARBEL-BEARD
The whisker-like barbels of the loach are used as feeling organs. This fish emerges from under stones after dusk to forage in the mud for worms, insects, and other small aquatic animals.

Water starwort provides cover for these shy loaches

Tiny river limpets attached to rock

CLAMPING DOWN
Under their rounded shells, the muscular feet of these tiny freshwater molluscs grasp this rock firmly.

The river's mouth

THE RIVER'S COURSE is ended. Its banks curl out to become the seashore, and the tidal influx of salt water begins to impose itself on the plant and animal life. The last stretch of a river is known as the estuary, and it is here that the river's currents slow down to a crawl and the smallest mud and silt particles, still in suspension, slowly settle on the bed and banks. The water, mixed by waves and tides, is often cloudy, so submerged plants are rare, since they do not receive enough light for photosynthesis (p.10). Relatively few plants and animals are adapted to the enormous variations in salt concentration, but those that are face little competition, so they are often found in huge numbers. The specimens shown below were all collected from an estuary, to give some idea of the range of animals and plants that can be found at the mouth of a river.

MOULTED FEATHERS
Discarded feathers are a common find on the estuary. They are evidence of the different bird species that live there.

Moulted feathers

Washed-up bone

Gull

ESTUARY GULL
The rich animal life of the estuary attracts gulls of all kinds.

DISCARDED SKELETONS
Among the fascinating items you can find washed up on the edge of the estuary are various bones.

Glasswort

Sea spurge

GLASS FROM PLANTS
The glassworts are so named because in former times their ashes (being high in soda) were used to make glass. They are common on estuaries and salt marshes (p.60), and in some places people pick their leaves to pickle or cook and eat.

CREEPING ABOUT
The sea spurge's creeping stem spreads through the sand dunes at the river's mouth. Like glasswort, it has thick, fleshy leaves.

DINNER-TIME AT LOW TIDE
Flocks of oystercatchers and other waders crowd on to the estuary mud at low tide, pecking and probing for worms, shrimps, shellfish, and crabs.

Fleshy leaves store water

Glasswort

Sea sandwort

Eel grass

Feathers

Roots begin to stabilize estuary mud

ESTUARY DUMP
The calmer waters of the estuary's tidal inlets are nature's dumping ground for all kinds of seaside debris, from dried-out seaweeds and eel grass to feathers, bits of weeds, and dead crabs.

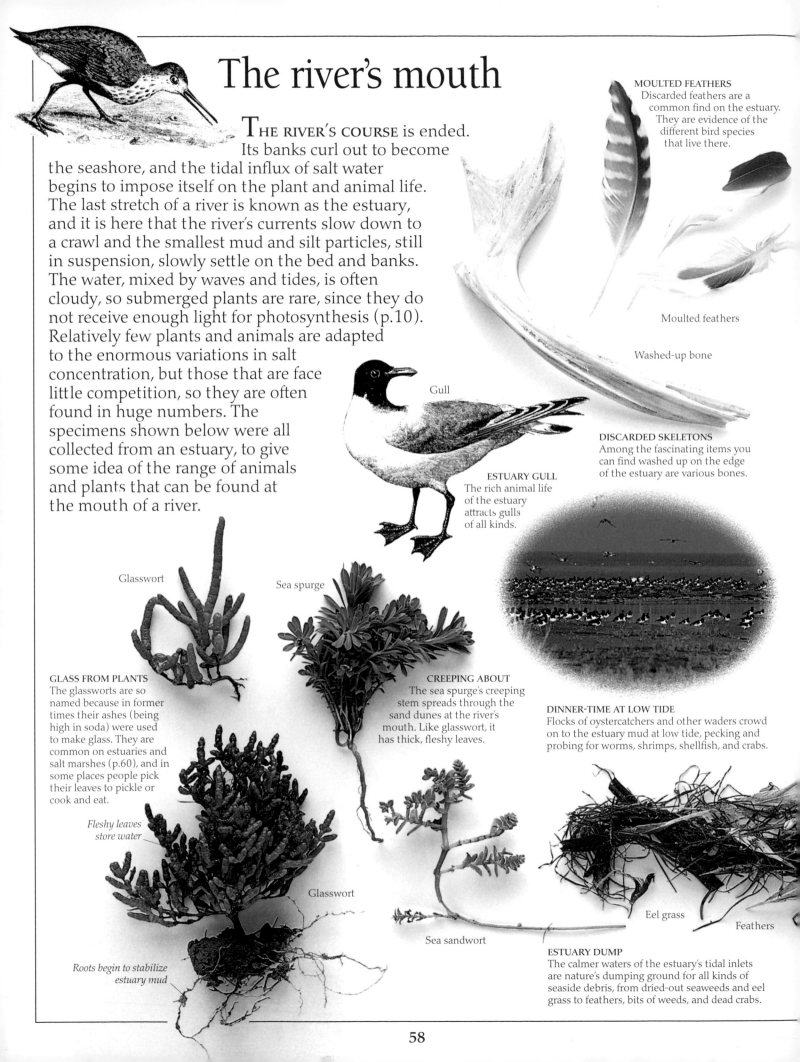

A LOT TO LEARN
Oystercatcher chicks hatch from eggs laid in the open or in short vegetation around the estuary. Oystercatchers feed by probing the mud with their long bills in search of molluscs, then prising open the shells or hammering a hole in them. The chicks can take up to six months to learn these specialized feeding techniques from their parents.

Oyster shell

Tellin shell

Cockle shell

Hole pecked by bird

Cockle shell

Tellin shell

Oystercatcher and chick

Winkles

Tellin

Cockle

Periwinkle

Mussel

Young crab

HOLE IN ONE
These mollusc shells have been pecked through by estuary birds, and the animals inside have been eaten.

UNDER THE BREAKWATER
Any obstruction on the flat estuary, such as a breakwater or pier, soon becomes colonized by a variety of life that can withstand the fluctuating salinity. The sea slater is a crustacean – a cousin of the woodlouse, and also a relative of the crab.

Sea slater

Lugworm

SHORE WORM
Squiggly casts on the estuary mud mark the position of a lugworm's U-shaped burrow.

Oyster shell

Slipper limpet

Cockle shell

Barnacles

Razor shell

IN FROM THE SEA
The shells of true seashore molluscs are often washed up on the estuary shore, as was this small barnacle encrusted stone, loosened by a storm.

Shelduck and chick

SHELDUCK DUCKLING
Young shelducks look like typical ducklings, but the adults bear more resemblance to geese than ducks. This waterfowl eats not only shellfish, but also fish, worms, and other small animals.

Crab

Dorsal fin

Pipefish

PIPEFISH
This relative of the seahorse has hardened outer skin and moves by mainly using its dorsal (back) fin. It copes well in the fluctuating salinity of estuary water.

Spiral wrack

SHORE WEED
In the more sheltered and seaward sites, shore algae can gain a foothold. This spiral wrack is characteristic of the upper shore zone.

The salt marsh

Many estuaries (p.58) are flanked by a broad expanse of land, riddled with creeks and channels, the salty soil supporting its own distinctive plant population. This is the salt marsh, and it is a very forbidding habitat for plants. Twice each day, sea water pours through the drainage channels and its salt soaks into the soil and mud. As the tide retreats, evaporation leaves behind a salty residue. Spring tides flood the entire marsh with sea water. Yet a few hours later, at low tide, heavy rain may have turned the surface into an almost freshwater habitat. The plants growing on a salt marsh have become specially adapted to such fluctuating conditions.

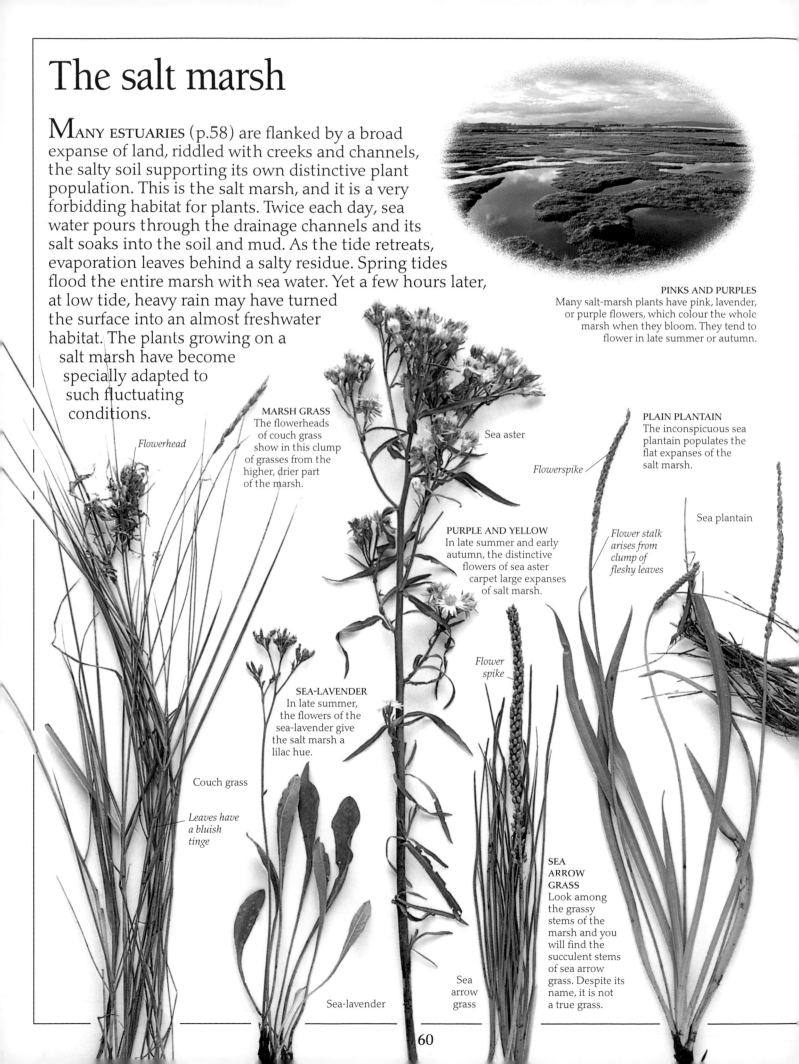

PINKS AND PURPLES
Many salt-marsh plants have pink, lavender, or purple flowers, which colour the whole marsh when they bloom. They tend to flower in late summer or autumn.

Flowerhead

MARSH GRASS
The flowerheads of couch grass show in this clump of grasses from the higher, drier part of the marsh.

Sea aster

PLAIN PLANTAIN
The inconspicuous sea plantain populates the flat expanses of the salt marsh.

Flowerspike

PURPLE AND YELLOW
In late summer and early autumn, the distinctive flowers of sea aster carpet large expanses of salt marsh.

Sea plantain

Flower stalk arises from clump of fleshy leaves

Flower spike

SEA-LAVENDER
In late summer, the flowers of the sea-lavender give the salt marsh a lilac hue.

Couch grass

Leaves have a bluish tinge

SEA ARROW GRASS
Look among the grassy stems of the marsh and you will find the succulent stems of sea arrow grass. Despite its name, it is not a true grass.

Sea-lavender

Sea arrow grass

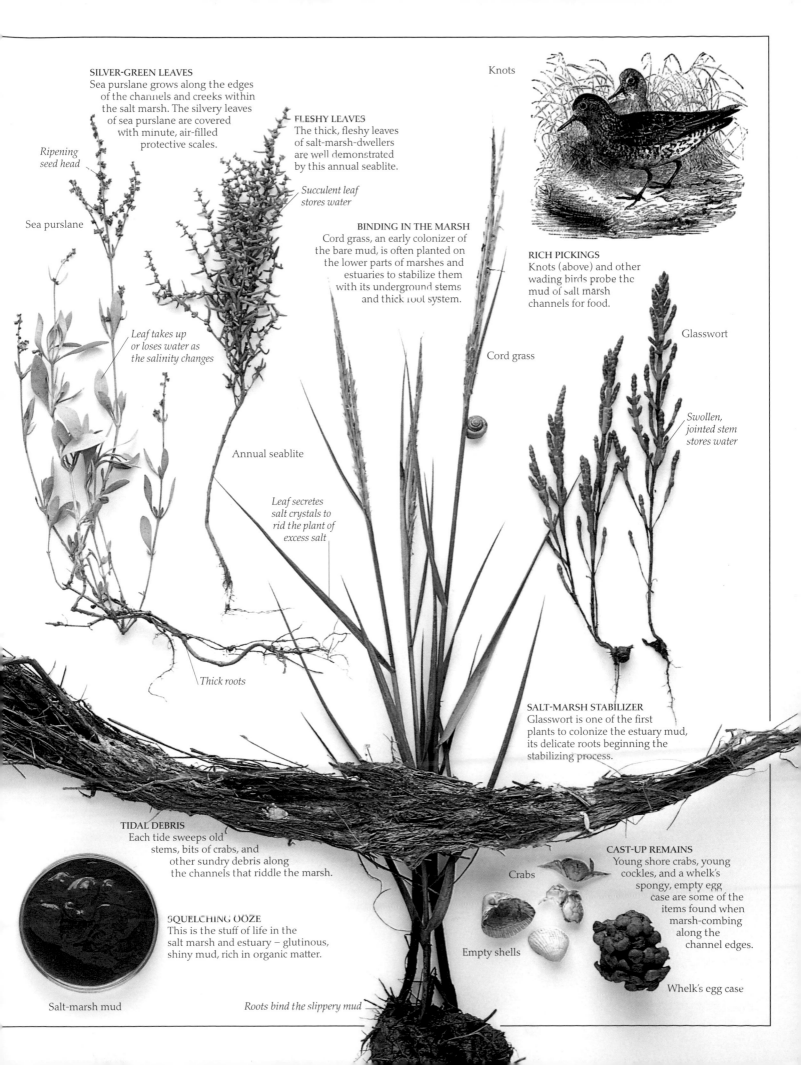

SILVER-GREEN LEAVES
Sea purslane grows along the edges of the channels and creeks within the salt marsh. The silvery leaves of sea purslane are covered with minute, air-filled protective scales.

Ripening seed head

Sea purslane

FLESHY LEAVES
The thick, fleshy leaves of salt-marsh-dwellers are well demonstrated by this annual seablite.

Succulent leaf stores water

BINDING IN THE MARSH
Cord grass, an early colonizer of the bare mud, is often planted on the lower parts of marshes and estuaries to stabilize them with its underground stems and thick root system.

Knots

RICH PICKINGS
Knots (above) and other wading birds probe the mud of salt marsh channels for food.

Leaf takes up or loses water as the salinity changes

Cord grass

Glasswort

Swollen, jointed stem stores water

Annual seablite

Leaf secretes salt crystals to rid the plant of excess salt

Thick roots

SALT-MARSH STABILIZER
Glasswort is one of the first plants to colonize the estuary mud, its delicate roots beginning the stabilizing process.

TIDAL DEBRIS
Each tide sweeps old stems, bits of crabs, and other sundry debris along the channels that riddle the marsh.

CAST-UP REMAINS
Young shore crabs, young cockles, and a whelk's spongy, empty egg case are some of the items found when marsh-combing along the channel edges.

Crabs

SQUELCHING OOZE
This is the stuff of life in the salt marsh and estuary – glutinous, shiny mud, rich in organic matter.

Empty shells

Salt-marsh mud

Roots bind the slippery mud

Whelk's egg case

Study and conservation

THE FASCINATING WILDLIFE OF PONDS AND RIVERS is suffering in our modern world. Pollution, demand for housing or farming land, and more people using the water for relaxation and recreation are all taking their toll. Conserving and preserving our natural freshwater habitats is increasingly important. It begins with study and understanding. Students of nature are interested in what lives where and why – learned through observation rather than interference. When out on a field trip, they have respect for nature, follow the country code, and obey the wildlife laws. If you wish to become involved in pond and river conservation, find out which organizations work in your local area.

THE MICROSCOPIC WORLD
A drop of pond water may look clear, but under a microscope such as this, it will be teeming with tiny water plants and animals. Magnification of about 20x to 200x is most common.

Magnifying glasses

LOOKING THROUGH LENSES
Magnifiers enable you to identify small water creatures or examine a flower's structure. A 10x lens is about right.

Field guide

Screw-top glass jars

Note pad

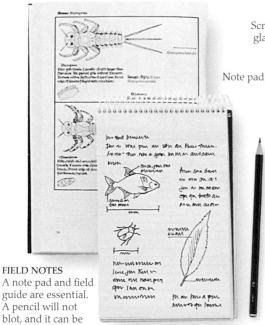

SHORT-STAY HOMES
Screw-top glass jars are useful for temporary storage and examination. Do not leave animals and plants in them for long.

SPOON AND BRUSH
These pieces of equipment enable small, delicate plants and animals to be transferred for study, and then replaced without harm.

DISHES AND DROPPERS
These allow small items to be moved gently and studied without too much disturbance.

Plastic spoons

Brush

Glass dish

Dropper

FIELD NOTES
A note pad and field guide are essential. A pencil will not blot, and it can be sharpened carefully with a pocket knife.

FARM WASTE
Accidental spillage of pig slurry into this river killed fish such as chub, dace, and roach – and thousands of smaller animals.

Digital camera in protective plastic underwater casing

DAMP-PROOF SNAPS
Waterproof camera housings (cases) allow photographs to be taken with an ordinary camera even in the spray of a fast stream. Photos record nature without disturbing it.

The dangers of pollution

Ponds, rivers, and other freshwater habitats are under constant threat of pollution. Fertilizers, pesticides, and other farming chemicals are washed through the soil by rain and into watercourses, where they may adversely affect the balance of nature. Industrial wastes discharged from factories into rivers can damage water life for long stretches downstream. Most authorities have clean-water laws, but these are not always observed; accidents happen, and inspectors cannot monitor every backwater. We can all contribute, by reporting suspicions to the authorities, volunteering to help clean out and restock a weed-choked pond, or clearing a stream used as a rubbish tip.

Folding pocket knife

Secateurs

Plastic bags and ties

Fine-mesh sieve

IN THE BAG
Aquatic plants dry out quickly in air. Keep them wet during transit in plastic bags.

A CLEAN CUT
Take plant samples only if you have permission, and use a sharp blade to minimize the damage.

Fork

Trowel

Sealable plastic containers

SIEVE FOR SORTING
A fine-mesh sieve can be rocked gently in water to sort small animals from mud and silt.

TAKING A SAMPLE
A bucket on a string can be tossed from a bridge, bank, or boat to sample the water.

SPLASH-PROOF CONTAINERS
Pack animals carefully in sealable containers, using waterweed as padding to minimize splashing.

SMALL DIGGERS
If you are permitted to dig up plants or search for muddy-bottom creatures, use a clean, sharp fork or trowel, and take great care.

Water-sampling bucket

Large-mesh net

Fine-mesh net

NET RESULTS
Nets have different mesh sizes, for large or small specimens. Exercise caution, so as not to uproot plants. After sorting, replace the net's contents in the water as quickly as possible.

Did you know?

AMAGING FACTS

The oldest recorded goldfish lived to the ripe old age of 43. On average, goldfish can survive for 20 to 30 years, and a well-kept koi (from the carp family) can live for about 50 years.

Mayflies, found near rivers and ponds, are sometimes called dayflies because of their short lifespan. After spending up to three years under water as nymphs, adult mayflies often die just a few hours after maturing, and rarely live for more than a few days. This is because the adults do not have functioning mouths or digestive systems, and therefore cannot feed.

Newts sometimes migrate long distances to breed. They often travel back to the pond where they grew up, finding their way by sight and smell.

The largest dragonfly that has ever existed was *Meganeura monyi*, which lived about 250 million years ago. Discovered as a fossil in France, it had a wingspan of more than 75 cm (30 in) – about four times the size of today's record-holder!

Historically, Native Americans in North America have found many uses for pond lilies. The roots were used medicinally, applied externally to wounds, and eaten to cure digestive ailments. The roots, leaves, and buds of the plant were also used for food, and even the seeds were fried and eaten, or ground into flour.

Pond lilies were once eaten as food

Tympanum

Tree frog

Like mammals, frogs have ears on the sides of their heads, but the eardrum, or tympanum, is outside instead of inside the skull. A frog's call is very loud for the animal's size, which raises the question as to how a frog avoids bursting its own eardrums. It may be because a frog's ears are connected to its lungs, so that the vibrations created by its call are felt not just in the eardrums, but throughout the body.

There are more than 4,000 species of frog and toad.

The cane toad (*Bufo marinus*) lays 35,000 eggs a year, more than any other amphibian.

Duckweed

The world's muddiest river is the Huang He (Yellow River) in China, which deposits silt over its flood plain and delta, covering an area of 141,645 sq km (54,690 sq miles). It is estimated that 2 billion tonnes of silt is deposited annually.

The smallest flowering plant in the world is *Wolffia angusta*, a species of duckweed that is found in Australia. With each plant measuring just 0.8 mm (0.031 in) long and 0.4 mm (0.015 in) wide, a tablespoon can hold up to 100,000 of them. It's no surprise that duckweed also holds the record for the world's smallest fruit. Measuring about 0.25 mm (0.01 in) long, these fruits weigh just 70 micrograms (0.00002 oz), which is about 4 billion times lighter than the world's biggest fruit, the squash.

The River Kenai, Alaska, USA, was home to the world's largest salmon, which weighed 44 kg (97 lb).

River otters sometimes travel across land in search of a mate. They move by running a few steps and then sliding on their bellies. One slide can be as long as 6 m (20 ft), with the otter reaching speeds of up to 29 kph (18 mph).

Fishing bats have echolocation so sophisticated that they can detect a minnow fish's fin as fine as a human hair protruding only 2 mm (0.08 in) above a pond's surface.

A lethal skin disease caused by the chytrid fungus (*Batrachochytrium dendrobatidis*) is threatening the survival of many of the world's amphibians. First identified in 1998, chytrid disease has been blamed for the extinction of around 40 species since 1980. The rapid spread of the disease is thought to be due to the global transport of amphibians for the pet trade and for food. When an infected frog arrives in a new location and then escapes, a rapid decline of local frog populations soon follows, since the native amphibian populations have no defences against the new fungus.

If there is a population explosion of the microscopic pond plants known as algae, it can cause great harm to the other pond inhabitants by exhausting the available oxygen supplies. Without enough oxygen, the pond's plants and animals will soon die.

Q What's the difference between a pond and a lake?

A A pond is a body of water that is shallow enough to support rooted plants, is fairly even in temperature all over, and is usually covered in mud at the bottom because the water is generally still. A lake is bigger than a pond and is too deep to support rooted plants, except near the shore. Some lakes are big enough for waves to be produced and may vary significantly in temperature from top to bottom. A pond is small enough to freeze solid during very cold winter spells, whereas a lake may freeze over at the surface, but it is unlikely to freeze completely solid.

Q Do frogs have teeth?

A Most frogs do have teeth of a sort. They have maxillary teeth, a ridge of very small teeth around the upper edge of the jaw, and vomerine teeth, tiny teeth on the roof of the mouth. However, because most frogs have no teeth on the lower jaw, they can only grip and not chew their food, which they have to swallow whole. Toads, on the other hand, have no teeth at all.

Q What is the largest freshwater fish?

A The giant pirarucu (*Arapaima gigas*), a native of the Amazon and Orinoco rivers in South America, is the largest fish in the world to dwell solely in fresh water. The heaviest recorded specimens weighed about 200 kg (440 lb). Also called the Amazon Redtail (because of the bright crimson colour of its tail) and the arapaima, this fish is caught for its meat. Its rough scales are used as sandpaper and nail files by local people. Due to overfishing, this species is now endangered, and international trade has been banned to help the stock to recover. As part of a conservation project, pirarucu have been transported to lakes in Malaysia and Thailand, where they grow to 50 kg (110 lb).

The pirarucu – the largest freshwater fish

Q What is the fiercest freshwater predator?

A The piranha fish is probably the most ferocious freshwater animal you can find. Native to the River Amazon, these fish have very powerful jaws and razorsharp teeth, and they can strip a carcass in seconds. Piranhas have been known to attack animals as large as goats. There are many different types of piranha, however, and not all are carnivorous. Some are vegetarian and eat no meat at all. Even meat-eating piranhas eat only fruits and nuts for much of the year. Native Americans use the jaws of piranhas to create tools for cutting wood and hair.

Q Can pond snails breathe underwater?

A No, but they can hold their breath for sustained periods of time. A pond snail takes in air from the surface of the pond using a special hole in its body. Above the water line, this hole sucks in air into its lung, but underwater the hole seals up.

Q How can you tell if a pond or river is polluted?

A Water quality is most accurately measured by scientific tests, which determine factors such as pH levels, clarity, and temperature. However, even without conducting any tests, the presence or absence of plant and animal life can act as indicators of pollution. If a habitat is unhealthy, insects are the first to disappear. Mayflies, stoneflies, and some types of beetle are particularly sensitive to pollution. Fish such as trout and minnows can only live in clean water, whereas goldfish and carp are more hardy and can survive some types of pollution. Most plants cannot grow in unclean waters.

Piranha

Record breakers

SMALLEST FISH
• The smallest living fish is the tiny *Paedocypris progenetica*, which lives in acidic swamps on the island of Sumatra, Indonesia. Discovered in 2005, it measures less than 8 mm (0.31 in) in length.

MOST SHOCKING FISH
• The electric eel (*Electrophorus electricus*), native to the River Amazon in South America, can stun or kill its prey with a single electric shock.

BIGGEST FROG
• The body of the African goliath frog (*Conraua goliath*) measures 30 cm (12 in) in length, and its outstretched legs add another 40 cm (16 in).

LONGEST RIVER
• The River Nile in Africa is the longest in the world, at 6,825 km (4,241 miles).

LARGEST RIVER SYSTEM
• The Amazon in South America is by far the biggest river system in the world. Its drainage basin covers an area of almost 6.2 million sq km (2.4 million sq miles).

HIGHEST WATERFALL
• Angel Falls, on the River Churún in Venezuela, South America, drops 979 m (3,212 ft) from Devil's Mountain.

Around the world

POND AND RIVER ENVIROMENTS vary greatly from continent to continent, and from climate to climate. Tiny ponds in Europe have very different plant and animal life to that found in the mighty River Amazon in South America or the frozen ponds of northern Canada. Here are some examples of the amazing flora and fauna that can be found in freshwater environments in different regions. Your local natural history museum is a great place to discover more examples for yourself.

AFRICAN FISH EAGLE
The predatory African fish eagle (*Haliaeetus vocifer*) is common in Africa, and is usually found near rivers and coasts. It feeds mainly on fish and amphibians, but in some areas it also preys on flamingoes and other waterbirds.

PINK FRESHWATER DOLPHIN
One of only four freshwater species of dolphin in the world, the pink dolphin (*Inia geoffrensis*), or boto, is found in the Amazon and Orinoco rivers in South America. It has a hump on its back instead of a fin and is a very intelligent animal. Humans are the only real predators of this species, and due to overfishing and destruction of its habitat, the survival of the pink dolphin is now endangered.

Dolphins have very sharp teeth

WESTERN POND TURTLE
The Western pond turtle (*Clemmys marmorata*) is only found in the states of Washington, Oregon, and California in the USA. These creatures can live for up to 50 years. They are extremely shy and will quickly hide at the first sign of human presence.

Western pond turtles like to bask in the sunshine during warmer months

THAI WATERFALL
This is one of the many waterfalls in Phu Kradung nature reserve in northern Thailand. The river shown here runs down a mountain that rises 1,325 m (4,240 ft) above sea level, and the aquatic habitat high up the mountain is unusual in Thailand's tropical climate. The cool temperatures at the top of the mountain mean that many of the plants are those of a temperate climate, and include pine forests and maple trees.

Arctic lichen by a frozen pond in Canada

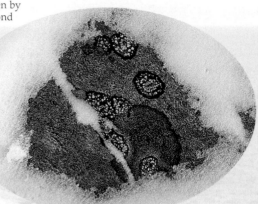

ARCTIC LICHEN
There are almost 1,000 types of Arctic lichen growing in North America. Lichens are partnerships between fungi and algae. They can survive for up to 5,000 years, withstand great extremes of temperature, and grow on almost any surface, including rock, tree bark, bones, and animal dung. Lichens are the chief winter food of moose and caribou.

This toad is an excellent swimmer, but it can only crawl on land, not hop

AFRICAN CLAWED TOAD
The African clawed toad (*Xenopus laevis*) has existed for about 125 million years. Native to sub-Saharan Africa, these toads spend most of their lives in water and very little on land. During dry spells, they can submerge themselves in mud without moving or eating for periods of up to a year, while they wait for rain to fall.

ÉTANG DE BERRE
The Étang de Berre (Berre Pond) is part of the delta of the River Rhône in the South of France. In recent years, this habitat has suffered severe pollution as a result of heavy industry in the area. This has had disastrous consequences for plants and animals that live in and around the water.

Find out more

THERE ARE MANY WAYS to find out more about pond and river life. If you live near a pond or river, you can study the changes that a freshwater habitat undergoes through the seasons. Using a notebook and camera, record the different plant and animal life that you come across. A natural history museum will contain information about the history and evolution of species. A day out fishing or following a riverside trail will allow you to observe and enjoy the teeming life of an aquatic habitat. You can also breed your own fish and grow plants in an aquarium at home.

GO FISHING
A visit to an angling shop will provide you with all the kit you need. Accompanied by an adult, set up in a calm spot beside a river or large pond on public land. Find out if you need permission and a licence before you fish, and also make sure it is not the close season, when fishing is not allowed so that the fish can breed undisturbed. When you catch a fish, always release it back unharmed into the water.

STUDYING FROGSPAWN
One of the most fun ways to explore pond life is to chart the growth of frogspawn into adult frogs. Spring is the season to look for frogspawn, which is created when a male frog fertilizes eggs laid in the water by a female. The eggs are protected by jelly, which floats to the surface. After about two weeks, the spawn will hatch into tadpoles, which continue to develop for several weeks before they reach adulthood.

Frogspawn

The spawn of one female common frog can contain up to 3,000 eggs

Pond surfaces are often overgrown with lilies

POND LIFE
Find out where your nearest pond is. You may know someone who has a pond in their back garden, or it might involve a trip to a local park or nature reserve. Both man-made and natural ponds are miniature worlds, alive with plants, fish, insects, and frogs. Use a notebook to record the species you find there.

RIVERSIDE TRAIL
There are many official riverside walks. Your local conservation society will have more details. The trail shown here is the Thames path in England, which starts in the Cotswold hills and ends at the Thames Barrier in London.

Thames map

HOME AQUARIUM
Rearing fish as pets in a freshwater aquarium can be very rewarding. This tank is a cold water aquarium containing an array of goldfish, including the common goldfish, the comet, or single-tailed goldfish, and fancy (fan-tailed) goldfish. An aquarium also allows you to grow aquatic plants. Fish and plants must be well cared for on a daily basis.

USEFUL WEBSITES

• Have fun designing your own virtual fish and aquariums!
www.virtualfishtank.com

• The Wildfowl & Wetlands Trust works to save wetlands in the UK and worldwide. Its website has details of the WWT's visitor centres, downloadable factsheets, and a Kids' Zone.
www.wwt.org.uk

• A guide to identifying the tiny lifeforms that live in ponds.
www.microscopy-uk.org.uk/pond/index.html

• Information on all aspects of keeping fish in aquariums; its FishKidz Corner page has tips, games, and a quiz.
www.fishchannel.com/fishkidz

NATURAL HISTORY MUSEUM
Any natural history museum will house exhibits of both preserved and living plant and animal specimens from pond and river habitats. These students and their teacher are studying living fire-bellied toads and their tadpoles.

Places to visit

CAIRNGORM NATIONAL NATURE RESERVE, SCOTLAND, UK
Aquatic attractions at Britain's largest nature reserve include a working fish farm where you can feed the trout, and fishing facilities.

AIGAS DAM FISH LIFT, AIGAS, SCOTLAND, UK
The dam has a specially constructed fish ladder to allow Scottish salmon to make their way upstream. A viewing facility allows visitors to watch the salmon pass through.

MARGAM RIVERBANK POND CENTRE, NEATH PORT TALBOT, WALES, UK
A fascinating exhibition that tells the story of a river from spring to sea, covering the flora and fauna of local freshwater environments.

NATURAL HISTORY MUSEUM, SOUTH KENSINGTON, LONDON, ENGLAND, UK
With exhibitions dedicated to fish, amphibians, plants, fossils, ecology, and birds, the life galleries hold plenty in store for eager students.

THAMES PATH NATIONAL TRAIL, UK
Running from the source of the river in the Cotswolds to the Thames Barrier, London, this amazing riverside trail covers 288 km (179 miles). Part of the trail can be covered in one day, or a family holiday could be organized around the walk.

ENVIRONMENTAL EDUCATION CENTRE, KELHAM ISLAND CENTRE, SHEFFIELD, UK
School education sessions covering pond and river life centred on the River Don, its weir, and a waterwheel built in 1210!

A school visit to the Natural History Museum, London, UK

Glossary

ALGAE Microscopic plants that grow in sunlit water containing nutrients such as phosphates and nitrates. Algae, like all aquatic plants, add oxygen to the water and are an important link in the food chain.

AMPHIBIAN A class of cold-blooded vertebrates, typically gill-breathing in the larval state and lung-breathing or skin-breathing as adults.

ALLUVIUM Sediment or loose material comprised of clay, silt, sand, gravel, and larger rocks deposited by moving water.

APPENDAGE An attached feature to the body of an animal.

AQUATIC Organisms that live or grow in a watery environment.

ARTHROPOD An animal with a segmented body and joined appendages; arthropods include crustaceans and insects.

BACTERIA Microscopic organisms without chlorophyll that multiply by simple division, and that often feed on dead organisms.

BARBEL A freshwater fish of the carp family, and the name for whisker-like appendages that act like feelers in certain fish's mouths.

BIVALVE An animal with a shell in two parts, or valves, such as an oyster.

Creeping jenny, a hardy plant

An estuary – the end of a river's journey

BRACT A small, leaf-like flap that grows just beneath a flower.

CANAL A constructed open channel for transporting water.

CARNIVORE An animal or plant that feeds on flesh.

CHLOROPHYLL The green pigment present in most plants and central to the process of photosynthesis.

CRUSTACEAN A member of a large class of arthropod animals with hard shells, such as crabs, lobsters, shrimps, and barnacles.

DORSAL FIN The fin at the back or rear of a fish's body.

ECOSYSTEM A community of organisms and their environment.

EROSION The wearing away of rock or soil by the gradual detachment of soil or rock fragments by water, wind, and ice.

ESTUARY The wide, lower, tidal part of a river where it flows into the ocean.

FROND A leaf or leaf-like structure, especially relating to palms and ferns.

FRY Young fishes just hatched, or a young salmon in its second year of life.

GASTROPOD A class of assymetrical molluscs, including limpets, snails, and slugs, in which the foot is broad and flat and the shell, if any, is in one piece and conical.

Pond snail, a gastropod

GRAVEL A loose natural collection of rounded rock fragments on a riverbed.

HABITAT The physical environment in which a plant or animal normally lives.

HARDY Relating to plants that can withstand extremes of temperature, including frost.

HERBIVORE An animal that eats only grass or other plants.

HERMAPHRODITE A plant or animal with the organs of both sexes.

INSECTIVORE An animal that feeds only on insects.

LARVA An animal in a developing or immature state that is markedly different from the full adult state.

LATERAL LINE A series of sensory pores along the side of a fish. The lateral line can detect water currents, vibrations, and pressure.

MAMMAL A large class of warm-blooded vertebrates that suckle their young and generally have a covering of hair.

MARGINAL Plants that grow around the edge of water.

METAMORPHOSIS The series of changes that an insect undergoes between its early life and adulthood. Insects that undergo incomplete metamorphosis change gradually as they grow up. Those that undergo complete metamorphosis change abruptly, during a resting stage called a pupa. In both types of metamorphosis, growth normally stops once the adult stage is reached.

MONOTREME A mammal that reproduces by laying eggs. Unlike other mammals, monotremes have a single opening for their reproductive and digestive systems.

NYMPH An immature form of some insects, such as mayflies or dragonflies; nymphs are similar to the adults, but with underdeveloped sex organs, and only sometimes with wings.

ORGANISM A living thing.

OMNIVORE An organism that feeds on both animal and plant food.

OVERWINTER When plants or animals stay alive throughout the winter season.

PARR A young salmon of up to two years of age, before it becomes a smolt.

PECTORAL FIN The anterior, or front-facing, pair of fins on a fish.

PERENNIAL A plant that lasts or flowers for more than two years.

PULMONATE An organism that has lungs, or similar organs.

PETAL One of the brightly coloured leaf-like parts of a flower.

PHOTOSYNTHESIS The process by which plants generate their own food. The food is created when a green pigment called chlorophyll reacts with sunlight, carbon dioxide, and water to make carbohydrates, water, and oxygen.

PHYTOPLANKTON The plant-like component of plankton, consisting mainly of microscopic algae.

PLANKTON Minute organisms, including animal and algae, that are found in the surface layers of water. Plankton drift with the current.

Trout only survive in freshwater habitats

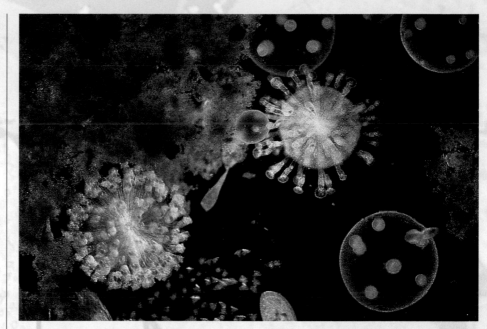

Phytoplankton, visible only under a microscope

POLLINATION The process by which pollen is carried from one flower to another. The male pollen fertilizes the female ovule and creates a seed. Insects or animals often carry pollen between flowering plants, or it can be blown by the wind.

PUPATION A passive stage in the development of an insect from larva to adult.

RAPIDS Fast, swirling currents that form where river water flows down a steep slope.

RHIZOME A creeping underground stem. Rhizomes often sprout leaves as they push their way through the ground.

SEPAL A leafy flap that protects a flower while it is still a bud. Sepals often fall off when the flower opens.

SMOLT A young salmon ready to migrate from fresh water to the sea; a smolt has a bluish upper body and silvery sides.

SOURCE The starting point of a river, usually from a natural water spring that emerges at high altitudes from inside the Earth.

SPAWN A mass of eggs laid in water, such as those laid by frogs.

STYLE The slender part of a flower that connects the stigma, which receives the pollen, and the ovary, which produces eggs.

TRIBUTARY A stream that flows into another stream, river, or lake.

VERTEBRATE Any animal that has a backbone. This group includes mammals, fish, birds, reptiles, and amphibians.

VENTRAL FIN Either of the paired fins on the belly of a fish.

WATERFALL A vertical cascade of water where a river plunges over hard rock.

YEARLING A one-year-old fish.

The source of a river is often very small

Index

Acknowledgements

Dorling Kindersley would like to thank the following:

The Booth Museum of Natural History, Brighton, UK
Ed Wade and Respectable Reptiles, Hampton, UK, for help with the amphibians and reptiles
Richard Harrison and Robert Hughes, Upwey Trout Hatchery for help with the trout eggs
Anne-Marie Bulat for her work on the initial stages of the book

Artwork Fred Ford and Mike Pilley of Radius Graphics, and Ray Owen
Design assistance Carole Ash, Neville Graham, Marytn Foote
Special photography Kim Taylor, p.27; Dave King, pp.2–5, 28–31, 36–37, 52–53, and 62–63
Consultancy David Burnie
Index Jane Parker
Proofreading Caitlin Doyle
Wallchart Peter Radcliffe, Steve Setford
Clipart CD Jo Little, Lisa Stock, Claire Watts, Jessamy Wood

The author would like to thank the following:

Don Bentley for loan of equipment; Mike Birch of Mickfield Fish Centre, Max Bond and Tim Watts of Framlingham Fisheries; CEL Trout Farm, Woodbridge; Keith Chell and Chris Riley of Slapton Ley Field Centre; Wendy and David Edwards, Ellen and Chris Nall, Jacqui and Tony Storer for allowing their ponds to be sampled; David Gooderham and Jane Parker for help with collecting; Andrea Hanks and staff at Thornham Magna Field Centre; Alastair MacEwan for technical advice; Ashley Morsely for fish care; Richard Weaving of Dawlish Warren Nature Reserve; John Wortley, Andy Wood and Anglian Water Authority.

Picture credits
The Publishers would like to thank the following for their kind permission to reproduce their photographs:

(Key: a-above; b-below/bottom; c-centre; f-far; l-left; r-right; t-top)

Heather Angel: 43tr, 45br, 53br; G I Bernard/Oxford Scientific Films: 51cl; B Borrell/Frank Lane Picture Agency: 39c; David Boyle/Animals Animals/Oxford Scientific Films: 66b; Bridgeman Art Library: 34tr; British Museum/Natural History: 48tl; Jane Burton/Bruce Coleman Ltd: 64bl; B B Casals/Frank Lane Picture Agency: 39t; John Clegg: 47cl; G Dore/Bruce Coleman Ltd: 48cr, 60tr; Fotomas Index: 39cl; EPA/Press Association Picture; Library: 67bl; Mary Evans Picture Library: 22tl, 23tr, 30bl, 40tr; C B and D W Frith/Bruce Coleman Ltd: 41br; Tom and Pam Gardener/Frank Lane Picture Agency: 38br; D T Grewcock/Frank Lane Picture Agency: 62br, 71br; Mark Hamblin/Frank Lane Picture Agency: 39bc; David Hosking/Eric and David; Hosking: 27, 37cl; E & D Hosking/FLPA – Images of Nature: 67c, 70b; Zig Leszczynski/Oxford Scientific Films: 65bl; Mansell Collection: 13c, tr, cl, 35cl, 49br, 42bl W Meinderts/Foto Natura/FLPA– Images of Nature: 65tr; The Natural History Museum, London: 69b;

Oxford Scientific Films: 71t; Fritz Polking/FLPA – Images of; Nature: 67tl; Dr Morely Reed/Science Photo Library: 39bl; Jany Sauvanet/Natural History Photographic Agency: 40cl; Richard Vaughan/Ardea: 58cr; Alan Weaving/Ardea: 66tl; Roger Wilmshurst/Frank Lane Picture Agency: 29t; Norbert Wu/Still Pictures: 66c

Illustrations by Coral Mula:
34bl; 35tl, 35cl; 36cl, 36bl, 36br; 38cl, 38c; 39ct

Wallchart:
Getty Images: Oleksandr Ivanchenko/Photographer's Choice ftr; Andy Rouse/The Image Bank cla (kingfisher)

Jacket:
Front: David Plummer/Dorling Kindersley: tl; all other images: DK Images. *Back* (all images): DK Images

All other images © Dorling Kindersley
For further information see:
www.dkimages.com